COOK'S
QUICK FROM
SCRATCH

EDITED BY OLGA RIGSBY

PENNINGTON PUBLISHING, INC.

PUBLISHED BY PENNINGTON PUBLISHING, INC.
2710 NORTH AVENUE
BRIDGEPORT, CONNECTICUT 06604

ISBN: 0-936599-10-3

LIBRARY OF CONGRESS CATALOG CARD NUMBER
89-63377

CONTENTS

Introduction
5

Appetizers and
Light Meals
9

Soups
33

Pasta, Grains, and
Breads
55

Seafood
83

Meat
113

Poultry
129

Vegetables
147

Salads
173

Cookies and Cakes
195

Desserts
207

Beverages
235

Credits
249

Index
254

INTRODUCTION

The best quick cooking is naturally fast. Fresh, high-quality ingredients are combined with a minimum of preparation, without substitutions and without short-circuit techniques that make a two-hour recipe into a streamlined hybrid.

This is also, by definition, healthy cooking, emphasizing juicy fruit desserts, simple soups, quick pastas, and main course salads. Sizzled salmon, a Cajun shrimp sandwich, or chicken salad with thyme and red-onion vinaigrette are all fast, fresh, and full of robust, natural flavors.

All of these recipes can be prepared in less than one hour and most in less than 45 minutes. This is quick cooking for the 1990s — fast, fresh, and flavorful.

ACKNOWLEDGEMENTS

Quick From Scratch has hundreds of authors from around this country—American chefs and cooks who have contributed to the pages of COOK'S from 1980 to the present. Their love of food and range of experience make this a very special cookbook.

Our thanks also go to Olga Rigsby who edited this volume and to Vicki Shearer and Julia Sharpe who assisted her. We are grateful to Stephen Doyle of Drenttel Doyle Partners in New York City who designed this volume, and Mimi Laaksonen, Cara Formisano, and Tracy Alia who worked long hours to make this project a reality.

Christopher Kimball
Publisher & Editorial Director

Appetizers and Light Meals

Appetizer Toasts
with Two Toppings
10

Tomato and
Parmesan Cheese
Topping
11

Herbed Olive
Topping
12

California Crostini
13

Crostini with Grilled
Summer Vegetables
and Smoked
Mozzarella
14

Fennel with
Olive Oil
15

Bacon and Tomato
Pita Pizzas
16

Walnut Gougère
17

Pâte à Choux
18

Cherry Tomatoes
Filled with Goat
Cheese and Thyme
19

Watercress
Cucumber
Sandwiches
20

Asparagus and
Ham Omelets with
Blue Cheese
21

Basic Omelet
22

Sour Cream,
Smoked Salmon,
and Black Caviar
Omelet
23

Apple Omelet
24

Apple Filling
25

Orange and Yogurt
Waffles
26

Onion and Fennel
Frittata
27

Savory-Swiss Chard
Frittata
28

La Piperade
29

Buttermilk
Cornmeal Pancakes
30

rusty rounds of toasted French bread can

be spread with a choice of two strongly-flavored, Mediterranean-style

toppings. For a party, guests can even assemble their own toasts.

½ loaf French bread (½ pound)
½ cup olive oil
Herbed Olive and Tomato and
    Parmesan Cheese Toppings
    (recipes follow)

PREPARATION AND COOKING Cut bread into eighteen ½-inch thick rounds. Lightly brush the top of each round with oil, place on a baking sheet, and toast in a 400°F oven until golden on the top and crisp throughout, 7 to 8 minutes. (Can store toasts in an airtight container for 2 weeks.)

SERVING Follow topping recipes for assembly and serving instructions.

MAKES **18** TOASTS

TOMATO AND PARMESAN CHEESE TOPPING

*T*he appetizer toasts can be capped with this classic tomato and cheese spread. The dried tomatoes provide an intense, vibrant flavor which is enhanced by the crustiness of the toasts.

9 sun-dried tomatoes in oil *or* dried tomatoes
1½ ounces Parmesan cheese
1 large garlic clove
9 appetizer toasts (recipe precedes)

PREPARATION Plump dried tomatoes in 2 cups hot water until softened, about 20 minutes. Remove dried tomatoes from their oil (or water) and put them into the workbowl of a food processor fitted with the metal blade; pulse until minced. Transfer to a small bowl. Can cover and refrigerate up to 2 weeks.

ASSEMBLY AND SERVING Adjust oven rack to high position and heat broiler. Thinly slice the Parmesan cheese. Peel and rub the garlic clove over the toast rounds. Spread 1 teaspoon minced tomato on each, top with cheese slices, and broil until cheese melts, about 2 minutes. Sprinkle with parsley and transfer toasts to a serving platter. Serve immediately.

MAKES **9** TOASTS

HERBED OLIVE TOPPING

If herbes de Provence *are not available, a similar mixture can be made by combining equal proportions of dried thyme, oregano, savory, rosemary, and fennel seed.*

1 medium shallot
1 small garlic clove
½ cup Kalamata olives
1 tablespoon capers
1 teaspoon dried *herbes de Provence*
1 tablespoon olive oil
½ teaspoon red-wine vinegar
9 appetizer toasts (recipe on page 10)

MAKES 9 TOASTS

PREPARATION Peel and mince the shallot. Peel the garlic. Pit the olives. Put the garlic, olives, capers, herbs, oil, and vinegar in the workbowl of a food processor fitted with the metal blade. Process mixture to a fine paste, about 1 minute. Transfer olive paste to a small bowl and stir in the shallots. (Can cover and refrigerate up to 3 weeks.)

ASSEMBLY AND SERVING Spread ½ tablespoon olive paste on each toast round and transfer to a serving platter.

*C*rostini are tiny open-faced sandwiches served as appetizers or antipasti. In Italy, they are topped with fine-chopped chicken livers or seafood, but this recipe is a California variation using tomato, garlic, olives, basil, and pungent asiago cheese. They make fine hors d'oeuvres.

1 cup loose-packed basil leaves, chopped coarse

1 medium tomato, seeded and chopped coarse

2 medium garlic cloves, minced

15 Kalamata olives, pitted and chopped coarse

2¼ ounces grated asiago cheese (¾ cup)

½ loaf French bread, cut into ¼-inch thick slices

PREPARATION Mix all ingredients but bread. Put bread slices on a baking sheet and spread each with ½ tablespoon of the olive mixture.

SERVING Heat broiler and toast crostini until golden brown and cheese bubbles, about 3 minutes. Serve immediately.

MAKES **12** CROSTINI

CROSTINI WITH GRILLED SUMMER VEGETABLES AND SMOKED MOZZARELLA

Cook crostini and serve them as appetizers while the main course is on the grill. If you do not have a covered grill, cover the baking pan with foil so that the vegetables stew, not sauté.

3 tablespoons butter

2 tablespoons olive oil

1 medium onion, sliced thin

2 medium carrots, peeled and julienned

1 medium green bell pepper, sliced thin, lengthwise

1 medium garlic clove, minced

2 small yellow squash, sliced thin, diagonally

4 medium plum tomatoes, peeled, seeded, and cut into medium dice

1/2 cup basil *or* parsley leaves, minced

Salt and ground black pepper

1/4 pound smoked mozzarella cheese, grated (1 cup)

1 loaf French bread, cut into sixteen 1/2-inch thick slices

COOKING: Heat the grill. Heat butter and oil in a 9- by 2-inch metal baking pan set in center of upper grill rack. Open vents halfway at bottom of grill and on lid. Add onions and carrots to pan; cover grill and cook until onions soften, about 5 minutes. Add peppers and garlic; cover grill and cook until peppers begin to soften, about 3 minutes. Add squash and tomatoes; cover grill and cook until all vegetables are just tender, about 4 minutes longer. Stir in basil; season with 1/2 teaspoon salt and 1/4 teaspoon pepper or to taste. Sprinkle cheese over vegetables; cover and cook until cheese melts, about 3 minutes. Remove baking pan from grill, cover with aluminum foil, and keep warm. Arrange bread slices around the cooler edges of the grill. Toast, turning once, until golden, about 1 minute.

SERVING Transfer grilled bread to a serving platter. Top each slice with a portion of the grilled vegetables and serve immediately.

MAKES **8** SERVINGS

Season this simple dish with coarse ground black pepper and serve with imported green olives.

1 large fennel bulb (1¼ pound)
¼ cup olive oil
Salt and ground black pepper

PREPARATION AND SERVING Trim fennel and discard outer leaves; trim fronds and reserve for another use. Cut bulb in half lengthwise; cut each half into 8 wedges. Arrange fennel on a serving platter; sprinkle with oil, ½ teaspoon salt, and ¼ teaspoon pepper. Serve chilled or at room temperature.

MAKES 8 SERVINGS

BACON AND TOMATO
PITA PIZZAS

ita bread makes a quick crust for these pizzas. A green salad is all that is needed to make these into a meal.

1 medium red onion

2 medium tomatoes

16 slices bacon (1 pound)

6 ounces fontina cheese

6 whole-wheat *or* white pita breads
   (6 inches in diameter)

2 tablespoons olive oil

2 tablespoons minced basil

1/4 teaspoon hot red-pepper flakes

PREPARATION Peel and cut 6 thin slices from onion; separate into rings. Thinly slice tomatoes. Halve bacon slices crosswise. Grate cheese (1 1/2 cups).

COOKING AND SERVING Adjust oven rack to middle position and heat oven to 450°F. Fry bacon in a large skillet over medium-high heat until crisp and brown, about 7 minutes. Remove bacon and drain on paper towels; discard drippings. Arrange pita breads, concave side up, on a large baking sheet. Brush with olive oil; sprinkle with basil and red-pepper flakes. Top each pita with equal amounts of onion rings, tomato slices, and bacon pieces. Sprinkle with grated cheese. Bake until cheese melts and bubbles, about 8 minutes. Serve immediately.

MAKES 4 SERVINGS

T*he gougère is a traditional Burgundian snack to accompany a glass of red wine. This variation adds walnuts, a perfect complement to the cheese.*

³/₄ cup walnuts

¹/₄ pound Gruyère cheese (³/₄ cup grated)

1 egg

¹/₂ teaspoon salt

¹/₂ batch Pâte à Choux (recipe follows)

¹/₂ teaspoon ground black pepper

¹/₈ teaspoon grated nutmeg

PREPARATION Chop the walnuts. Grate the cheese.

COOKING Butter and flour a baking sheet, or butter and line with parchment paper. Draw a 9-inch circle on the piece of parchment or, if you butter and flour the sheet, draw a circle in the flour. Beat egg with a pinch of salt for egg wash. Heat oven to 425°F.

Make the Pâte à Choux. Stir salt and pepper, nutmeg, ¹/₂ cup of the grated cheese, and ¹/₂ cup of the walnuts into it. Using a pastry bag fitted with a ¹/₂-inch plain tip, pipe the dough around the circle in 1¹/₂-inch mounds that just touch each other, or drop mounds around the circle from a spoon, or pipe 24 separate 1-inch mounds. Lightly brush the top of the wreath or individual mounds with egg wash and strew with remaining cheese and walnuts. Bake until well puffed, about 15 minutes. Do not open door while cooking. Lower heat to 350°F and continue baking about 15 minutes more. Prick side of each puff and return to oven for 5 minutes. Serve warm or at room temperature.

MAKES ONE 9-INCH WREATH OR 24 SMALL PUFFS

PATE A CHOUX

~

Also known as cream puff pastry, pâte à choux is quick to make from simple ingredients. It is equally good with either sweet or savory fillings.

6 tablespoons water

3 tablespoons unsalted butter

⅛ teaspoon salt

½ cup flour

2 eggs at room temperature

PREPARATION In a saucepan, combine the water, butter, and salt. Bring to a boil over medium heat to melt the butter. Remove pan from heat, add flour, and beat to combine. Return to heat and cook, stirring constantly, until the paste forms a ball and leaves the sides of the pan, about 1 minute. Continue cooking until a thin film forms on the bottom of the pan, about 2 minutes. Turn off heat. Make an indentation in the center of the dough, crack an egg into the well, and beat the paste until smooth. Make an indentation again and proceed in the same way for the remaining egg.

MAKES ENOUGH DOUGH FOR THE WALNUT GOUGERE

herry tomatoes are also wonderful with

stuffings such as olive pesto, corn salad, pastina or orzo, crab salad,

vinaigrette, or sour cream and caviar.

3 ounces fresh goat cheese (6
    tablespoons)

3 ounces cream cheese (6
    tablespoons)

¼ cup heavy cream

25 cherry tomatoes (about 1 pint)

25 lemon thyme leaves plus several
    additional sprigs

PREPARATION Bring the cheeses to room temperature and beat cheeses with the heavy cream until the mixture is smooth. (Can cover and refrigerate up to 3 days.) Rinse, stem, and remove the bottom third of each cherry tomato, then use a melon baller or a small spoon to remove the seeds and ribs. Invert and drain the hollowed out tomatoes on paper towels for 10 minutes.

ASSEMBLY AND SERVING Bring the cheese filling to room temperature. Transfer tomatoes to a serving plate. Using a pastry bag fitted with a ¼-inch star tip, pipe filling into each tomato. (Can cover and refrigerate up to 4 hours.) Top tomatoes with thyme leaves and garnish platter with thyme sprigs.

MAKES **25** STUFFED TOMATOES

These delicate sandwiches are perfect for afternoon tea as well as for outdoor picnics.

1 seedless cucumber
½ bunch watercress (about 2½ ounces or ⅓ cup minced)
3 ounces cream cheese
8 thin slices white bread
Salt and ground black pepper

PREPARATION AND SERVING Cut the cucumber into very thin slices. Trim stems from watercress. Wash, dry, and mince the watercress and combine with cream cheese. Trim crusts from bread. Spread all 8 slices of bread with the watercress and cream cheese. Arrange cucumber slices on top of 4 slices of the bread, season with salt and pepper, and cover with a slice of bread. Cut into small triangles. Recipe can be prepared to this point several hours ahead and refrigerated.

MAKES **16** SANDWICHES

ASPARAGUS AND HAM OMELETS WITH BLUE CHEESE

O*melets are simple to prepare, and on-hand ingredients make delicious fillings. Blue cheese is an assertive addition to the quick omelets.*

4 medium scallions

8 medium asparagus

4 ounces blue cheese

Salt

8 eggs

1 teaspoon Dijon-style mustard

2 tablespoons butter

4 thin slices baked ham (4 ounces)

PREPARATION Thinly slice scallions, including green tops ($^1/_2$ cup). Remove and reserve asparagus tips. Cut stalks into $^1/_2$-inch pieces, discarding the tough ends. Crumble the blue cheese.

COOKING Heat oven to 200°F. Bring 3 quarts water to boil in a large saucepan. Add 1 teaspoon salt and asparagus tips and stems. Cook until bright green and tender, about 3 minutes. Drain, refresh, and drain again; set aside. Beat eggs with 1 tablespoon water, the mustard, and 1 teaspoon salt. Stir in scallions. Heat $^1/_2$ teaspoon butter in a 7-inch, nonstick omelet pan. Add about $^1/_2$ cup of the egg mixture; cook over medium heat, stirring until eggs just begin to set, about 1 minute. Top the eggs with a ham slice and sprinkle with a quarter of the asparagus and the cheese. Fold the omelet in half, then slide onto a heatproof platter; keep warm in the oven. Repeat with remaining omelet ingredients, adding butter to pan as necessary.

SERVING Transfer omelets to warm dinner plates and serve immediately.

MAKES **4** SERVINGS

*N*othing beats a creamy omelet as the high-lighted main course or dessert for a luncheon, brunch, or supper. Omelets are a snap — actual cooking time can be as little as 60 seconds.

2 *or* 3 eggs
1 tablespoon water
Pinch ground black pepper
Pinch salt
**2 teaspoons unsalted butter plus
    more for top of omelet**

PREPARATION In a bowl, beat eggs with water until well combined. Add salt and pepper.

COOKING In an omelet pan over medium-high heat, melt 2 teaspoons butter until bubbly. Pour in eggs and stir with flat side of fork, shaking pan with your other hand until eggs form a creamy mass. Grasp pan handle with your right hand and hit your right arm with the fist of your left hand to slide eggs toward edge of pan. Using the back of a fork, fold bottom half of omelet up. Grasp pan handle from underneath, with your fingers on top of handle. Invert pan toward you to turn omelet onto a plate. If you choose, reshape omelet into an oval with a clean towel. Rub a teaspoon or so of butter on top and serve immediately.

MAKES ❶ OMELET

SOUR CREAM, SMOKED SALMON, AND BLACK CAVIAR OMELET

*T*he basic omelet can ascend to sublime *heights when filled with caviar and smoked salmon.*

1 Basic Omelet (recipe precedes)

2 tablespoons sour cream

1 ounce smoked salmon, sliced very thin and then cut into 1/2-inch by 3-inch strips

1 tablespoon black caviar

Dill sprigs for garnish

SERVING Slit omelet down center. Spoon sour cream into slit and top with smoked salmon strips. Arrange caviar on top of salmon, garnish with dill sprigs, and serve immediately.

MAKES **1** OMELET

APPLE OMELET

This sweet omelet makes a delicious dessert or late-evening snack. It is satisfying in both taste and appearance.

2 eggs
2 teaspoons Applejack
2 teaspoons heavy cream
Pinch salt
1 tablespoon unsalted butter
⅓ cup Apple Filling (recipe follows)
Confectioners' sugar for topping

PREPARATION In a bowl, beat eggs until combined. Stir in Applejack, heavy cream, and salt.

COOKING In an omelet pan, heat butter until foamy. Pour in egg mixture. Stir with flat side of a fork until eggs form a creamy mass, shaking pan with your other hand. Hold pan with your right hand and hit your right arm with the fist of your left hand to slide eggs toward edge of pan. Put Apple Filling in center of omelet. Using the back of a fork, fold bottom half of omelet up over filling. Grasping pan handle from underneath with your fingers on top of handle, invert pan toward you and turn omelet onto a plate. Use a kitchen towel to reshape oval if necessary. Sprinkle with confectioners' sugar. Using a skewer heated over a burner for a few minutes, make a crosshatch design on top. Serve immediately.

MAKES **1** OMELET

APPLE FILLING

This tasty mixture of apples, lemon juice, brown sugar, cream, and Applejack is an ideal filling for a sweet omelet.

2 Golden Delicious apples, peeled and cut into ¼-inch-thick-slices (about 2 cups)

1 to 1½ teaspoon lemon juice

2 tablespoons unsalted butter

3 tablespoons dark-brown sugar

3 tablespoons Applejack

1 tablespoon heavy cream

½ teaspoon grated lemon zest

PREPARATION In a bowl, toss the peeled, cut apples with 1 teaspoon of the lemon juice.

COOKING In a skillet, melt butter until hot. Add apples and cook over medium-high heat for 1 minute, turning once. Stir in brown sugar. Cook over medium heat until dissolved, 3 to 5 minutes. Pour Applejack and cream into pan and cook until alcohol evaporates and sauce is reduced, 3 to 5 minutes. Add lemon zest and taste for seasoning. Add more lemon juice if necessary.

MAKES ENOUGH FILLING FOR 6 OMELETS

ORANGE AND YOGURT WAFFLES

≈

These tender waffles have a lovely wake-up orange flavor. The marmalade syrup is delicious, and if sweet, juicy blood oranges are available, they add color that is as good as the taste.

2 to 3 navel, Valencia *or* blood
    oranges

Orange Syrup
1 cup orange marmalade
1/4 cup blood, navel *or* Valencia
    orange juice, from above
1/2 lemon

6 tablespoons butter plus more
    for serving
1 3/4 cups flour
1/4 cup wheat germ
1 teaspoon baking powder
2 teaspoons baking soda
Salt
4 eggs
2 cups plain yogurt
2 tablespoons sugar
1/4 teaspoon grated nutmeg

PREPARATION Grate 1 tablespoon zest from the oranges. Squeeze 1/2 cup orange juice. *For the syrup*, put marmalade and 1/4 cup of the orange juice in a small saucepan. Squeeze 1 tablespoon juice from the lemon and add. Warm over low heat until the marmalade just melts. Melt 6 tablespoons of the butter. Combine flour, wheat germ, baking powder, baking soda, and 1/4 teaspoon salt in a bowl and set aside. Recipe can be prepared to this point a few hours ahead.

COOKING AND SERVING Heat waffle iron. Separate eggs. Beat the egg yolks until foamy. Beat in the yogurt, orange zest, remaining 1/4 cup orange juice, sugar, nutmeg, and melted butter. Gradually add the flour mixture, stirring until just blended. Beat the egg whites until they form soft peaks and then fold them into the batter. Pour batter onto the preheated waffle iron and cook until lightly browned. Heat Orange Syrup if cold. Serve waffles with butter and Orange Syrup.

MAKES 4 SERVINGS

T

ONION AND
FENNEL FRITTATA

he frittata is a simple dish, and yet the complementary combination of the fennel and the onion makes it special.

½ cup olive oil

3 large onions, sliced thin

2 fennel bulbs, sliced thin
    lengthwise

14 large eggs

Salt and ground black pepper

PREPARATION AND COOKING Heat oven to 425°F. Heat olive oil in a 2-quart baking pan over medium heat. Sauté onions until translucent, about 5 minutes. Remove onions from pan and sauté fennel over high heat until edges darken. Return onion to pan and arrange vegetables in pan. Set the pan aside. In a large bowl, beat eggs until well mixed but not fluffy. Pour eggs over fennel and onions. Sprinkle liberally with salt and pepper. Bake in center of preheated oven until puffed and golden brown and center is cooked through, 25 to 30 minutes.

SERVING Serve the frittata hot, warm, or at room temperature, cut into wedges.

MAKES **8** SERVINGS

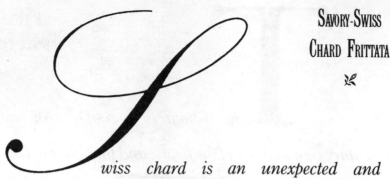

Swiss chard is an unexpected and tasty ingredient in this savory frittata, which is equally good served warm or at room temperature. Cut into wedges, it can be served as a party appetizer.

2 medium boiling potatoes

2 medium onions

4 ounces Gruyère *or* other Swiss
   cheese

3 tablespoons butter

7 eggs

¼ cup milk

¼ teaspoon cayenne pepper

Salt

¾ cup blanched Swiss chard

PREPARATION Slice potatoes ¼-inch thick. Thinly slice the onions (1 cup) and grate the cheese (1 cup).

COOKING Adjust oven rack to high position and heat broiler. Melt the butter in a 10-inch ovenproof skillet. Add the potatoes and sauté over medium-high heat until lightly browned, about 3 minutes. Add the onions and sauté until softened, about 2 minutes. In a medium bowl, whisk the eggs, milk, cayenne, and ½ teaspoon salt. Stir in the Swiss chard and cheese. Pour the egg mixture over the vegetables and cook, covered, over very low heat until the frittata bottom is set and the top is still slightly runny, 10 to 12 minutes. Broil frittata until the top is set and golden, about 2 minutes.

SERVING Cut frittata into wedges and serve immediately.

MAKES **4** SERVINGS

La Piperade

*T*his traditional combination of eggs, peppers, tomatoes and ham is a classic recipe of the Basque region, where the Pyrenees mountains separate Spain from France.

3 tablespoons olive oil

2 onions, diced

2 cloves garlic, crushed with ¹/₂ teaspoon coarse salt

2 large ripe tomatoes, cored, seeded, and diced

1 green bell pepper; stem, seeds, and ribs removed; diced

1 red pepper, stem, seeds, and ribs removed, diced

1 small hot pepper; stem and seeds removed, minced

¹/₄ teaspoon sugar

¹/₄ teaspoon black pepper

3 ounces cured ham, julienned

6 eggs

1 tablespoon chopped parsley for garnish

COOKING In a large, well seasoned or nonstick skillet, heat 1 ¹/₂ tablespoons of the olive oil. Add onions and garlic/salt mixture and sauté until onion is wilted, about 5 minutes. Add tomatoes, peppers, sugar, and black pepper. Stir. Cook covered, over medium heat until vegetables are very soft and mixture has thickened, about 25 minutes. Uncover, increase heat, and reduce mixture 1 to 2 minutes if necessary. Transfer to a large bowl and set aside. Clean pan. In clean pan, brown ham in remaining 1¹/₂ tablespoons olive oil for about 5 minutes over low heat. Remove ham with a slotted spoon and keep warm. Reserve oil in pan. In a bowl, beat eggs with a fork. Add eggs to reserved tomato mixture. Heat reserved oil in frying pan and pour in egg/tomato mixture. Simmer mixture, stirring, over low heat just until eggs begin to set. Stop stirring and let eggs continue to cook until set.

SERVING Spoon eggs onto serving plates. Top with warm ham and sprinkle with parsley.

MAKES 6 SERVINGS

T

his simple recipe results in pancakes whose outside crunch gives way to a golden, grainy interior.

1³/₄ cups yellow cornmeal

1¹/₂ teaspoons salt

³/₄ teaspoon baking soda

¹/₃ cup flour

2 eggs

2¹/₄ cups buttermilk plus more if necessary

¹/₃ cup light salad oil *or* up to 3 tablespoons bacon drippings plus oil to make ¹/₃ cup

Butter for serving

Boysenberry *or* raspberry syrup for serving

PREPARATION Heat a griddle or a cast-iron pan. Sift together cornmeal, salt, baking soda, and flour. In a bowl, mix eggs, buttermilk, and oil or drippings plus oil. Combine mixtures. Batter should be the consistency of heavy cream. If batter is too thick, add more buttermilk. Lightly butter hot griddle or pan and spoon batter onto surface in approximately 4-inch cakes. Cook over medium heat until bottom is golden brown. Flip and cook until second side is golden brown.

SERVING Top pancakes with butter and boysenberry or raspberry syrup.

MAKES **4** SERVINGS

SOUPS

Cold Nectarine
Soup
34

Brussels Sprouts
and Beer-Cheese
Soup
35

Potage Printanière
36

Red Snapper Soup
37

Red Snapper Stew
38

The Trellis
Cheese Soup
39

Tomato and
Garlic Soup
40

Red Snapper and
Garlic Sauce
41

Chilled Sugar-Snap
Pea Soup with Mint
42

Country Corn
Chowder
43

Fennel Soup with
Cheese
44

Peppery Lentil Soup
45

Corned Beef and
Cabbage Soup
46

Chilled Avocado
Soup with
Coriander Salsa
47

Chicken Soup with
Almonds
48

Sausage and
Succotash Soup
49

Summer Garden
Minestrone
50

Orange and
Carrot Soup
51

Smoky Sweet-
Potato Soup with
Sour Cream and
Jalapeños
52

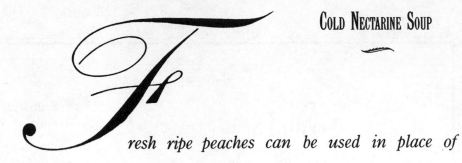

COLD NECTARINE SOUP

F *resh ripe peaches can be used in place of*
nectarines in this summertime soup.

8 nectarines

3 cups dry white wine

¼ cup honey *or* to taste

¼ cup lemon juice

**¼ teaspoon ground cinnamon *or*
to taste**

¼ cup plain yogurt

2 tablespoons chopped pistachios

PREPARATION Pit and coarsely chop nectarines without peeling
and put in a nonreactive saucepan. Add wine, honey, and
lemon juice and bring just to a boil. Remove from heat,
cover, and cool for 30 minutes. Puree the nectarine mixture
in a food processor or blend until smooth, working in
batches if necessary. Strain through a sieve, pressing with
the back of a spoon to extract all liquid. Discard the fibers.
Season to taste with cinnamon and a little extra honey if
needed. Chill thoroughly.

SERVING Ladle the nectarine soup into bowls, top each serving
with a dollop of yogurt, and sprinkle with pistachios.

MAKES **4** SERVINGS

B

BRUSSELS SPROUTS AND BEER-CHEESE SOUP

~~~

eer and cheese are great partners for the full-flavored brussels sprouts in this hearty soup, which is the perfect quick supper for a chilly evening.

½ pound brussels sprouts

6 slices bacon

1 onion, chopped

1 red bell pepper, diced

1½ cloves garlic, minced

2¾ tablespoons flour

1 teaspoon dry mustard

12 ounces beer

1½ cups chicken stock

7 ounces shredded cheddar cheese

Salt and ground black pepper

COOKING Cook brussels sprouts in boiling, salted water until just tender, 6 to 8 minutes. Drain, cut sprouts in half, and set aside. Fry bacon until crisp. Drain and crumble bacon. Reserve drippings. In bacon drippings, sauté onion, red pepper, and garlic over medium-low heat until softened, about 4 minutes. Stir in flour and mustard and cook, stirring, about 2 minutes. Slowly whisk in beer until mixture is smooth and bubbly, about 1 minute. Stir in stock, bring to a simmer, and continue cooking over low heat, stirring often, 5 to 7 minutes. Remove from heat and stir in cheese in four additions, stirring until cheese melts after each addition. Stir in sprouts and season to taste.

SERVING Ladle into soup bowls and garnish with bacon.

MAKES **4** SERVINGS

ou can vary this recipe by adding diced green beans, zucchini, or shredded greens of any kind. Coarser vegetables such as cabbage benefit from a sprinkling of cheese.

²/₃ pound green peas (about 1 cup *or*
    ¹/₄ pound shelled)

3 leeks

3 ribs celery plus leaves for garnish

¹/₂ head romaine lettuce (about ¹/₂
    pound *or* 4 cups)

1¹/₂ quarts chicken stock

Pinch of sugar

Salt and ground black pepper

Croutons

4 tablespoons butter

6 slices firm white bread

PREPARATION Shell the peas. Trim the leeks, leaving about 3 inches of green. Quarter lengthwise to just above the root end and rinse under cold water, fanning the layers. Cut leeks and celery into thin slices, reserving the celery leaves for garnish. Cut the lettuce leaves crosswise into strips. Bring stock to a simmer in a large saucepan over medium heat. Add the peas, leeks, celery, lettuce, and sugar and season to taste with salt and pepper. Reduce heat to low and cook, uncovered, until the vegetables are tender, about 15 minutes. *For the croutons*, melt the butter. Remove crusts and toast the bread. Brush both sides of bread with the butter, cut into ¹/₂-inch cubes, and wrap in foil.

COOKING AND SERVING Heat oven to 300°F. Bake croutons in foil in preheated oven until crisp and warm, about 10 minutes. Reheat soup if necessary, pour into bowls, and garnish with celery leaves. Pass croutons separately.

MAKES **8** SERVINGS

T

he licorice taste of Pernod and fennel combine perfectly in a light and elegant soup.

2 1½- to 2-pound red snappers
1 carrot
1 rib celery
1 leek, white part only
2 bulbs fennel
2 tomatoes
½ cup chopped parsley
½ cup chopped coriander
1 quart fish stock
1 cup white wine
¼ cup Pernod
¼ pound butter, cut in pieces
Salt and ground black pepper

PREPARATION Fillet the fish and make stock with the bones. Cut carrot, celery, leek, and fennel into ⅛-inch thick julienne strips. Peel, seed, and chop tomatoes. Chop parsley and coriander.

COOKING In a heavy pot, bring fish stock and wine to a boil. Add fish, reduce heat to low, and poach until just cooked through, about 5 minutes. Transfer fillets to 4 warm bowls and keep warm. Add vegetables to stock and cook until tender, about 2 minutes. Remove vegetables with a slotted spoon and divide among fish fillets. Add tomatoes to stock and cook for 2 minutes. Add Pernod and cook on low heat for 2 more minutes. Add parsley and coriander and swirl in butter. Season with salt and pepper to taste.

SERVING Pour soup over snapper.

MAKES 4 MAIN-COURSE SERVINGS

T*his robust soup is ample enough to serve as a main course. You can use any firm, white-fleshed fish in place of the snapper, and add clams or mussels for variety.*

6 tablespoons olive oil

8 shallots, halved

3 whole, tiny new potatoes *or* 2 red
    potatoes, cut into bite-size
    pieces

1 carrot, cut into bite-size pieces

1 red onion, sliced

1 bulb fennel, cut into bite-size
    pieces

Salt and ground black pepper

2 cups water

Juice of 1 orange

Juice of 1 lemon

1 sprig fresh sage *or* 1/4 teaspoon
    dried

1 sprig parsley

2 bay leaves

Zest of 1 orange, removed in strips

1 cup fish stock *or* clam juice

1 pound red snapper with skin
    intact, scaled, cut into 1-inch
    cubes

COOKING In a large skillet, heat 2 tablespoons of the olive oil. Sauté shallots, potatoes, carrot, onion, and fennel over medium heat until tender, about 6 minutes. Season lightly with salt and pepper and set aside. In a large saucepan, simmer water, orange and lemon juice, sage, parsley, bay leaves, and orange zest over low heat, skimming occasionally, for 30 minutes. Strain. Season to taste with salt and pepper. Add stock and remaining 1/4 cup olive oil and bring to a boil. Add snapper cubes and cook for 3 minutes. Add vegetables and cook until fish just tests done, about 2 minutes more.

SERVING To serve, ladle snapper and vegetables into individual warm bowls. Cover with hot fish stock.

MAKES **4** SERVINGS

There is nothing more comforting than a pot full of this gutsy soup simmering on the stove on a raw winter day.

4 tablespoons unsalted butter

3 tablespoons flour

1 tablespoon vegetable oil

1 onion, sliced

1 small carrot, cut into thin slices

1 rib celery, cut into thin slices

3 cups hot chicken stock

6 ounces shredded Oregon
  Tillamook cheddar cheese *or*
  other medium-sharp yellow
  cheddar

Salt and ground black pepper

COOKING AND SERVING In a heavy saucepan, melt butter. Add flour to make roux. Cook thoroughly over low heat, stirring often, about 10 minutes, being careful not to allow to color. Remove from heat and set aside. In a heavy skillet, heat oil and sauté onion, carrot, and celery over medium-low heat for 5 minutes until soft but not brown. Gradually add hot chicken stock to the cooked roux, stirring constantly, over medium heat until mixture is smooth and bubbly, 3 to 4 minutes. Simmer over low heat, 5 minutes, stirring often. Add sautéed vegetables to the soup and allow to simmer until vegetables are cooked, about 8 to 10 minutes, stirring often. Remove soup from heat, and gradually stir in shredded cheese. Continue to stir until all of the cheese has been added and soup is smooth. Season to taste with salt and pepper and serve immediately.

MAKES **4** SERVINGS

TOMATO AND GARLIC SOUP

~

This recipe suggests the use of new garlic — the immature, underdeveloped head pulled up from the ground in early spring. It looks like a scallion and has a definite garlic flavor.

1½ pounds fresh plum tomatoes *or* 16 ounces canned

1 large onion

1 new garlic (optional)

1 rib celery

2½ tablespoons fresh chopped basil *or* 1½ teaspoons dried

2 tablespoons butter

1 tablespoon olive oil

5 cloves regular garlic

3 cups chicken stock

Red Pepper and Garlic Sauce (recipe follows)

Chopped fresh basil *or* parsley for garnish

Salt and ground black pepper

PREPARATION Peel, seed, and quarter the tomatoes. Cut the onion, new garlic, and celery into thin slices. Chop 2½ tablespoons basil. In a large pot, heat the butter and olive oil over medium heat. Add the onion, new garlic, whole garlic cloves, celery, and basil and sauté until soft, about 8 minutes. Add the tomatoes and stock and simmer, covered, for 15 minutes. Remove from heat and puree in a food processor or food mill. Make the sauce. (Recipe can be made to this point several hours ahead.)

SERVING Mince basil or parsley for garnish. Reheat soup and season to taste with salt and pepper. Serve in soup bowls with a dollop of the Red Pepper and Garlic Sauce and a sprinkling of fresh basil or parsley.

MAKES **4** SERVINGS

RED PEPPER AND GARLIC SAUCE

❧

This contemporary version of the classic French sauce rouille is put together in a food processor instead of the traditional mortar and pestle.

1 red bell pepper
1 2-inch-thick slice French bread
4 large cloves garlic
2½ tablespoons olive oil
¼ teaspoon cayenne
Salt and ground black pepper

PREPARATION Char the pepper over a gas flame, under the broiler, or on the grill until skin is blackened. Peel, seed, and chop. Soak the bread in water to soften and then squeeze out all moisture. Puree the garlic and bell pepper in a food processor until almost smooth. Add the bread and process briefly. With the machine running, slowly add the olive oil. Season to taste with cayenne and salt and black pepper and process until very smooth. (The sauce can be made a few hours ahead.)

MAKES **1** CUP

CHILLED SUGAR-SNAP PEA SOUP WITH MINT

*M*int accents the garden-fresh flavor of this cold soup. You can make it a day ahead so that the flavors have more time to mellow. Since sugar-snap peas have a short season, you can use snow peas instead.

½ onion
1 pound sugar-snap peas
4 tablespoons butter
1½ cups chicken stock
5 cups half-and-half
1 cup sour cream
2 limes
Salt and ground black pepper
3 tablespoons chopped ginger mint
   or other fresh mint plus mint
   leaves for garnish

PREPARATION Chop onion. Remove strings from peas. Melt butter in a large pot, add the onion, and cook over medium heat until soft, about 3 minutes. Add peas and cook 5 minutes more. Add stock and bring to a simmer. Puree in a food processor, strain and chill. Whisk in the half-and-half and sour cream. Squeeze the lime juice and add. Season to taste with salt and pepper. The soup can be made a few hours ahead.

SERVING Chop 3 tablespoons mint and stir into the soup. Serve soup garnished with whole mint leaves.

MAKES 4 SERVINGS

W hen fresh corn is not in season, you can use frozen corn for this real, stick-to-the-ribs New England chowder.

½ mild yellow onion

2 ribs celery

3 peppercorns

¼ teaspoon dried thyme leaves

1 bay leaf

¼ teaspoon dried marjoram

2 parsley sprigs

1 small clove garlic

3 ears sweet corn *or* 1½ cups corn
   kernels

3 tablespoons bacon fat (from about
   ¼ pound bacon)

¼ cup flour

1 quart chicken stock

2 small potatoes

1 cup light cream

Salt and white pepper

Butter for garnish

PREPARATION Chop onion and celery. Crush the peppercorns. Tie the thyme, bay leaf, marjoram, parsley, peppercorns, and garlic in a cheesecloth bag. Cut the kernels from the cobs. In a large pot, heat bacon fat. Add onions and celery to the bacon fat in pot and sauté until soft, being careful not to brown, about 3 minutes. Sprinkle vegetables with flour and continue to cook over low heat, stirring frequently, for 10 minutes. Be careful not to brown. Add chicken stock to the pot and bring to a boil, stirring frequently. Meanwhile, peel and dice potatoes. Reduce heat to medium and add potatoes. Add herb bag to the simmering soup. Add corn and simmer until potatoes are tender, about 12 minutes. Add cream, return to a simmer, and season the chowder with salt and pepper to taste.

SERVING Pour chowder into soup bowls and garnish with a dollop of butter.

MAKES **4** SERVINGS

# FENNEL SOUP WITH CHEESE

ennel's strong, anise flavor and the rich-ness of the melting cheese make a truly distinctive soup.

2 pounds fennel (about 5 bulbs)

1 onion

1½ cups Gruyère cheese (½ pound)

2 tablespoons oil

Salt and ground black pepper

1 quart water, approximately

PREPARATION Trim the fennel bulbs and quarter. Remove and reserve core from each quarter. Set aside some fennel leaves for garnish. Cut bulbs and cores crosswise into thin slices. Halve the onion and cut into thin slices. Grate the Gruyère as fine as possible. In a large pot, heat the oil. Add the onion, fennel, and 1½ teaspoons salt. Sauté over high heat for 5 minutes. Add water as needed. Season to taste with salt and pepper and simmer until fennel is tender, about 15 minutes.

SERVING Add cheese gradually, whisking constantly, and season to taste with salt and pepper. Sprinkle with reserved fennel leaves and serve at once. (The cheese will become stringy if reheated.)

MAKES 4 FIRST-COURSE SERVINGS

*L*ike *dry beans, lentils are highly nutritious.*

But they cook more quickly than beans, and they don't require soaking.

1 clove garlic

1 small onion

2 fresh *or* canned plum tomatoes

1 small bunch fresh coriander
   (optional)

3 tablespoons oil

Salt and ground black pepper

1 tablespoon ground cumin

1 cup dry lentils

1 teaspoon oregano

1 teaspoon paprika

$\frac{1}{2}$ teaspoon cayenne *or* to taste

1 quart water

$\frac{1}{2}$ cup sour cream, approximately

PREPARATION Mince the garlic. Chop the onion. Peel, seed, and chop the tomatoes. Chop the coriander leaves.

COOKING Heat the oil in a large pot. Add the onion, sprinkle with about $\frac{1}{2}$ teaspoon salt, and cook over low heat until soft, about 3 minutes. Add the garlic and cook 30 seconds. Stir in the cumin and cook about 2 minutes until lightly toasted. Add the lentils, oregano, paprika, and cayenne and stir to coat with oil. Add water and tomatoes and bring to a simmer. Lower heat, season with salt and pepper, and cook, covered, until lentils are soft but not mushy, about 30 minutes. Adjust seasoning.

SERVING Reheat soup if necessary. Serve with a dollop of sour cream and sprinkle with coriander.

MAKES **4** FIRST-COURSE SERVINGS

S

avoy cabbage has a more delicate taste and more tender leaves than the widely available green cabbage.

1 small head savoy *or* green
    cabbage
1 clove garlic
6 tablespoons butter, approximately
$1/4$ teaspoon dried thyme leaves
$1^1/2$ tablespoons caraway seeds
    (optional)
Salt and ground black pepper
1 quart chicken stock
$1/2$ cup beer (optional)
$3/4$ cup shredded Swiss cheese
    (about $1/4$ pound)
$3/4$ pound thick-sliced corned beef
1 loaf crusty Italian bread

PREPARATION Remove the outer layers of dark cabbage leaves. Quarter, core, and slice the head into thin, short shreds. Mince the garlic.

COOKING Melt 4 tablespoons of the butter in a large pot and stir in the cabbage, garlic, thyme, caraway seeds, and about $1/2$ teaspoon salt. Cook over medium-high heat, stirring frequently, until cabbage is wilted, about 5 minutes. Add the stock and beer and bring to a simmer. Cook until cabbage is very tender, about 30 minutes. Shred the cheese and cut the corned beef into thin slices. Heat broiler. Cut eight $1/4$-inch thick slices of bread. Melt remaining 2 tablespoons butter and brush on both sides of each slice of bread. Put on a baking sheet and toast in preheated broiler just until golden on each side. Top slices with cheese and return to broiler until cheese is melted. Reheat soup if necessary. Add the corned beef to the soup. Just heat through and season to taste with salt and pepper.

SERVING Top the soup with cheese croutons at the last moment. Pass extra croutons as needed.

MAKES 4 SERVINGS

CHILLED AVOCADO SOUP WITH CORIANDER SALSA

*T*his cool and velvety soup relies on the natural sweetness and texture of ripe avocados. The red and green salsa flavored with coriander — also known as cilantro — adds a zesty touch.

Coriander Salsa

2 small tomatoes

1 two-inch piece cucumber

½ red bell pepper

1 jalapeño pepper

2 scallions

1 small clove garlic

1 tablespoon minced fresh
  coriander leaves

Pinch cumin

Salt

Soup

2 small avocados

4 teaspoons lemon juice

4 teaspoons lime juice

2 cups chicken stock

1⅓ cups light cream

Salt and ground black pepper

PREPARATION *For the salsa,* peel, seed, and chop the tomatoes and cucumber. Seed and chop bell pepper. Carefully remove seeds and ribs and then mince the jalapeño. Mince the scallions and garlic. Mince the coriander. Combine all salsa ingredients. Let stand at least 15 minutes at room temperature. *For the soup,* peel and pit the avocados. Puree the avocados in a food processor or food mill with lemon and lime juices. Add the stock, cream, and salt and pepper. Blend well, chill.

SERVING Pour the soup into bowls and put some salsa in the center of each serving.

MAKES **4** SERVINGS

lmonds, used both as an ingredient and as a crunchy garnish, add an unexpected flavor to chicken soup.

4 tablespoons butter

1 large clove garlic

6 tablespoons olive oil

1/2 cup sliced almonds

3 tablespoons minced chives *or* 2
scallions

3/4 cup parsley sprigs

1 tablespoon lemon juice

1/4 cup grated Parmesan

Salt and ground black pepper

3/4 pound boneless chicken

4 1/2 cups chicken stock

1/4 cup uncooked tubettini *or* other
small, dried pasta

PREPARATION Bring butter to room temperature. Mince the garlic. Heat 4 tablespoons of the oil in a large skillet and sauté the almonds over medium-low heat until almonds are golden, about 2 minutes. Add garlic and cook another minute. Remove and reserve about half of the almonds and garlic for garnish. Mince chives or scallions, green part only. Transfer remaining almonds and the oil from the skillet to a food processor. Wipe and reserve skillet. Add the parsley, chives or scallions, lemon juice, and butter to processor and pulse to a coarse puree. Grate the cheese and add it and 1/4 teaspoon salt to processor; blend. Cut chicken into pieces.

COOKING Bring stock to a boil and cook pasta in it until tender, about 8 minutes. In reserved skillet heat remaining olive oil. Season the chicken with salt and pepper and sauté over medium-high heat until golden, about 3 minutes. Add the chicken, pureed almond mixture, and reserved almonds and garlic to the soup. Season to taste.

MAKES 4 SERVINGS

SAUSAGE AND SUCCOTASH SOUP

*T*his Southern-style soup — somewhat like a gumbo — is a nourishing combination of homey vegetables flavored with sliced smoked sausage. Frozen lima beans, corn, and okra are good substitutes for the fresh vegetables.

½ pound lima *or* other shell beans

3 ears fresh corn *or* about 1½ cups corn kernels

¼ pound okra

1 onion

1 small red bell pepper

½ pound smoked sausage

3 tablespoons butter

3½ to 4½ cups chicken stock

Salt and cayenne pepper

PREPARATION Heat grill or broiler. Shell the beans. Run a knife down the center of all the rows of kernels of 2 ears of corn and scrape the kernels, releasing both the kernels and the milk into a bowl. Cut the kernels from the remaining ear of corn and add them to the bowl. Trim and cut the okra diagonally into ½-inch lengths. Chop the onion and seed and chop the bell pepper.

COOKING AND SERVING Prick the sausage and grill, 5 to 7 minutes (or longer for larger sausage), turning to brown all sides evenly. Cut the sausage into thin slices. In a large saucepan, heat the butter. Sauté the onion and bell pepper over medium heat until softened, about 3 minutes. Add the shelled beans, okra, and stock. Bring to a boil. Add the corn and simmer until vegetables are tender, about 5 minutes. Stir in the sausage slices and heat through. Season with salt and cayenne pepper to taste.

MAKES 4 SERVINGS

T ry this lively version of the classic Italian chunky vegetable soup. It is laden with fresh summer produce, and it tastes even better the second day.

6 plum tomatoes

1 leek

1 rib celery

1 carrot

1 clove garlic

1 green bell pepper

1/4 pound green beans

1 zucchini

1 yellow summer squash

1/2 pound savoy cabbage *or* regular
    cabbage (about 1/3 head)

3 tablespoons olive oil

6 1/2 cups beef *or* chicken stock

3 ounces broken vermicelli

1 tablespoon minced fresh
    marjoram *or* 1 teaspoon dried

1 tablespoon minced fresh basil *or* 1
    teaspoon dried

1 teaspoon minced fresh thyme *or*
    1/2 teaspoon dried

Salt and ground black pepper

Grated Parmesan cheese for serving
    (optional)

PREPARATION Peel, seed, and chop the tomatoes. Rinse the leek thoroughly. Slice the leek, celery, and carrot. Mince the garlic. Seed and dice the bell pepper. Cut the beans on an angle into 1-inch lengths. Slice the zucchini and summer squash and shred the cabbage. In a heavy saucepan, heat the olive oil over medium heat. Sauté the leek, celery, and carrot for about 3 minutes. Add the garlic, bell pepper, and tomatoes, and sauté about 2 minutes. Add the stock and bring to a boil. Add the beans, zucchini, squash, cabbage, and vermicelli. Return to a boil, add dried herbs if using, and cook until pasta is tender, about 5 minutes. Mince marjoram, basil, and thyme. Stir in fresh herbs. Season with salt and pepper.

SERVING Serve with Parmesan cheese on the side, if desired.

MAKES **4** SERVINGS

ORANGE AND CARROT SOUP

❧

This soup is good hot or cold, not only as part of a lunch or dinner menu, but also as an unusual starter for breakfast or brunch. Float a thin slice of orange on top for an attractive garnish. A sprinkle of coriander leaves adds a touch of color as well as flavor.

½ teaspoon minced fresh ginger
1 pound carrots (about 8)
4 scallions
2 tablespoons butter
3 cups chicken stock
Salt and ground black pepper
6 to 7 navel *or* Valencia oranges
2 tablespoons chopped fresh
    coriander for garnish

PREPARATION Mince the ginger. Cut carrots and scallions into thin slices. Melt the butter in a saucepan; add the ginger, carrots, and scallions and sauté over low heat until the scallions are soft but not brown, about 10 minutes. Add 2 cups of the chicken stock; season with salt and pepper, and simmer, covered, until the carrots are tender, about 10 minutes. Puree the mixture in a food processor or blender or press through a food mill. Return puree to the saucepan and add the remaining 1 cup chicken stock. Peel one of the oranges and cut four thin slices for garnish. Squeeze 1½ cups juice from remaining oranges and add to the saucepan. Season to taste with salt and pepper.

SERVING Heat soup if serving warm. Chop coriander. Float an orange slice on each serving and sprinkle with coriander.

MAKES 4 SERVINGS

SMOKY SWEET-POTATO SOUP WITH SOUR CREAM AND JALAPENOS

The smooth and sophisticated texture of this first-course soup contrasts wonderfully with its rough and exciting tastes. The sweetness of the potatoes is set off by the smoke of the bacon, while the jalapeños add a piquant jolt.

1 onion
1 large leek
2 cloves garlic
$1/4$ cup rendered bacon fat
2 sweet potatoes (about 1 pound)
$2^{1}/_{2}$ cups chicken stock, approximately
$1/4$ teaspoon dried thyme
Pinch of nutmeg
2 to 4 pickled jalapeños
$1/2$ cup light cream
Salt
$1/2$ cup sour cream

PREPARATION Chop the onion. Trim and mince the leek. Mince the garlic.

COOKING In a large pot, melt the bacon fat. Add the onion, leek, and garlic and cook, covered, over low heat, stirring once or twice, until very soft, about 15 minutes. Scrape mixture into a food processor or blender. Meanwhile, peel the sweet potatoes and cut into $1/2$-inch chunks. Add the sweet potatoes, chicken stock, thyme, and nutmeg to the pot. Bring to a boil, partially cover, and lower heat. Simmer, stirring occasionally, until the sweet potatoes are very tender, about 30 minutes. Cool slightly. Transfer the sweet potatoes to the food processor or blender with a slotted spoon, reserving the liquid. Puree until smooth. Add the reserved liquid and puree again. Trim and mince the jalapeños. Return the soup to the pot, add the light cream, and thin to the consistency desired with additional chicken stock.

SERVING Reheat soup, stirring often, until steaming. Season to taste with salt. Put the soup into warm bowls, garnish with sour cream and pickled jalapeño.

MAKES 4 SERVINGS

PASTAS, GRAINS, AND BREADS

Ravioli with Fresh
Tomato and Garlic
Sauce
56

Winter Vegetable
Pasta
57

Bow Ties with Spicy
Chicken and Sweet
Peppers
58

Vermicelli with
Zucchini and Salmon
59

Linguine with
Turkey and
Mushrooms
60

Ham and Orzo Salad
with Vinaigrette
61

Rigatoni with
Bacon, Tomato, and
Ricotta
62

Bow Ties with
Arugula, Bacon, and
Parmesan Cheese
63

Fusilli with Veal and
Artichokes
64

Risotto with Ham
and Asparagus
65

Risotto with
Artichokes
66

Quick Paella
67

Wehani Rice with
Port and Pecans
68

Mexican Fried Rice
69

Saffron Rice with
Sun-Dried
Tomatoes
70

Scallop and Bacon
Jambalaya
71

Oriental Pilaf
72

Lemon and Almond
Pilaf
73

Vegetable Oriental
Noodles
74

Popovers
75

Blueberry Corn
Muffins
76

Blue and Yellow
Cornsticks and
Muffins
77

Corn Muffins with
Spiced Ham
78

Saffron Cornbread
79

Herbed Potato
Biscuits
80

Herb Cheese
Biscuits
81

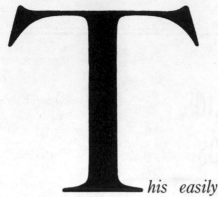

RAVIOLI WITH FRESH TOMATO AND GARLIC SAUCE

his easily prepared combination can be served as a first course, according to the Italian tradition, or as a light entrée at lunch or supper.

12 plum tomatoes

6 cloves garlic

²/₃ cup chopped parsley

¹/₂ cup black Mediterranean olives

¹/₄ cup olive oil

2 pounds fresh or frozen cheese ravioli

Salt and ground black pepper

Grated Parmesan cheese (optional)

PREPARATION Peel, seed, and chop the tomatoes. Mince the garlic. Chop the parsley. Halve and pit the olives. Heat the oil in a saucepan over medium heat. Add the garlic and cook until soft, about 3 minutes. Add the tomatoes, raise the heat to high, and cook about 10 more minutes. (Recipe can be done to this point a few hours ahead.)

COOKING AND SERVING Cook the ravioli in a large pot of boiling, salted water until tender, about 8 minutes. Drain. Meanwhile, reheat the garlic and tomato mixture if cold. Remove from heat, add the olives and parsley, and season to taste with salt and pepper. Top the ravioli with the garlic and tomato mixture. Serve with grated Parmesan cheese.

MAKES 4 SERVINGS

✗

*F*ennel imparts a wonderful anise flavor to this earthy dish, and the red pepper strips are a colorful accent. Try the optional truffles if you want a more elegant combination.

2 bulbs fennel, cut in half

3 cups heavy cream

6 black truffles (optional)

4 leeks, white and light green part only, cut in half, rinsed, and sliced

1 celery root, peeled and cut into $1/8$-inch slices

Salt and ground black pepper

12 ounces fettuccine

1 red bell pepper, seeded and cut into strips

Fresh chervil leaves (optional)

PREPARATION Remove hearts from fennel bulbs. Separate layers and cut into strips.

COOKING In a saucepan, bring cream to a boil. Reduce heat to a simmer and cook about 5 minutes. Turn off heat and add truffles if using, fennel, leeks, and celery root. Season to taste and let sit, covered, for $1/2$ hour.

SERVING Cook fettuccine, reheat vegetable mixture over low heat and add red-bell pepper strips. Serve sauce over fettuccine and garnish with chervil.

MAKES ❹ SERVINGS

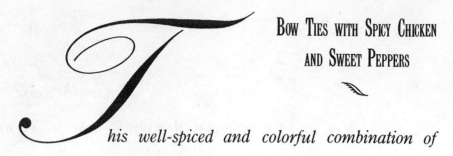

Bow Ties with Spicy Chicken and Sweet Peppers

*T*his well-spiced and colorful combination of chicken, vegetables and pasta is amazingly quick to make.

2 red bell peppers

1 large yellow bell pepper

½ clove garlic

2 boneless chicken breasts (about
 ¾ pound)

1 small lemon

¾ pound bow-tie pasta

6 tablespoons butter

1½ teaspoons chili powder

1½ teaspoons ground cumin

1½ teaspoons ground coriander

3 tablespoons white wine

¾ cup chicken stock

1½ teaspoons rice-wine vinegar

Pinch cayenne pepper

Salt and ground black pepper

PREPARATION Char the peppers over a gas flame, under the broiler, or on a grill until skin is blackened. Peel, seed, and cut peppers into thin julienne strips. Mince the garlic. Cut the chicken into 1-inch cubes. Squeeze juice from lemon. (Recipe can be made to this point a few hours ahead.)

COOKING Cook the pasta in a large pot of boiling, salted water until just tender. Drain and return to pot. Meanwhile, melt 3 tablespoons of the butter in a large frying pan. Add the peppers, chili powder, cumin, and coriander to the pan and sauté over medium-high heat for 2 minutes. Add the garlic and chicken and cook over medium heat for 5 minutes, stirring frequently. Add the wine, stock, lemon juice, vinegar, and cayenne pepper and bring to a boil. Whisk in remaining 3 tablespoons butter. Add sauce to the pasta, toss, and heat through. Season to taste.

MAKES **4** SERVINGS

VERMICELLI WITH ZUCCHINI AND SMOKED SALMON

✣

Smoked salmon is perfect for quick recipes because it requires no cooking. In fact, its flavor is spoiled when heated. Serve the pasta with a salad of green lettuce and arugula dressed with balsamic vinaigrette.

2 medium garlic cloves

1 medium zucchini (8 ounces)

6 ounces sliced smoked salmon

Salt

12 ounces vermicelli *or* other thin-strand pasta

4 tablespoons butter

1 cup heavy cream

2 teaspoons minced tarragon *or* 1/2 teaspoon dried

1 small lemon

1 tablespoon small capers, drained

Ground black pepper

PREPARATION Peel and mince garlic. Halve the zucchini lengthwise, scrape out seeds, and thinly slice crosswise. Cut smoked salmon into 1/4-inch strips.

COOKING Bring 6 quarts water to boil in a soup kettle. Add 1 tablespoon salt and the pasta; boil until tender, about 8 minutes. Drain, return to kettle, cover, and keep warm. Meanwhile, melt butter in a large skillet. Add garlic and zucchini; sauté until softened slightly, about 2 minutes. Add cream and tarragon; simmer until cream thickens slightly, about 3 minutes. Grate in 1 teaspoon lemon zest and squeeze in 1 tablespoon juice; season with salt to taste. Pour sauce over warm pasta; toss over low heat.

SERVING Transfer pasta to a warm bowl. Arrange strips of salmon over the pasta. Sprinkle with capers and 1/2 teaspoon black pepper; serve immediately.

MAKES **4** SERVINGS

Having sliced, sautéed turkey on hand gives you a good head start on a simple but delicious dinner.

2 medium onions

½ pound fresh mushrooms

2 medium plum tomatoes

2 tablespoons olive oil

2 cups cooked turkey

⅛ teaspoon dried thyme

⅛ teaspoon dried rosemary

⅛ teaspoon dried oregano

Salt and ground black pepper

½ cup dry vermouth *or* white wine

½ cup chicken stock *or* broth

⅛ teaspoon hot red-pepper sauce

12 ounces dry linguine *or* 9 ounces
    fresh

4 tablespoons softened butter

1 tablespoon minced parsley

PREPARATION Peel and thinly slice onions. Rinse and thinly slice mushrooms. Cut tomatoes into ½-inch dice.

COOKING AND SERVING Heat olive oil in a large skillet. Add the onions and mushrooms and sauté until softened, about 3 minutes. Add turkey, spices, ½ teaspoon salt, ¼ teaspoon pepper, tomatoes, and vermouth, and bring to a boil. Simmer for 2 minutes. Add chicken stock and simmer until sauce has reduced to ¾ cup, about 5 minutes. Stir in red pepper sauce. Cover and keep warm. Bring 6 quarts of water to a boil in a large soup kettle. Add 2 tablespoons salt and the pasta. Boil until pasta is tender about 9 minutes. Drain pasta and toss with butter and sauce over very low heat. Adjust seasoning. Sprinkle with parsley and serve immediately.

MAKES 4 SERVINGS

HAM AND ORZO SALAD WITH MUSTARD THYME VINAIGRETTE

T*iny, rice-shaped pasta ovals team up with smoked ham and colorful vegetables and are then enlivened by a sprightly mustard and thyme vinaigrette.*

Mustard-Thyme Vinaigrette

2 tablespoons white wine vinegar

2 teaspoons coarse grain mustard

1 garlic clove, minced

1 tablespoon minced fresh thyme *or*
    1 teaspoon dried

Salt and ground black pepper

3 tablespoons olive oil

3 tablespoons vegetable oil

Ham and Orzo Salad

Salt

1 cup orzo

12 ounces fully cooked smoked
    ham, cut into medium dice

2 plum tomatoes, seeded and cut
    into medium dice

1 cup frozen corn kernels, thawed

8 scallions, sliced thin, crosswise

1/2 medium red bell pepper, cut into
    medium dice

1 large celery stalk, sliced thin

8 red leaf lettuce leaves

PREPARATION *For the vinaigrette,* mix first 4 ingredients plus 1/2 teaspoon salt and 1/2 teaspoon pepper in a medium bowl. Gradually whisk in oils; set aside.

COOKING *For the salad,* bring 2 quarts water to boil in a large soup kettle. Add 2 teaspoons salt and the pasta; cook until tender, about 8 minutes. Drain and rinse under cold running water; drain again. Add the next six ingredients and vinaigrette; toss to coat; adjust seasonings.

SERVING Line a serving platter with lettuce leaves. Transfer salad to platter and serve immediately.

MAKES 4 SERVINGS

RIGATONI WITH BACON, TOMATO, AND RICOTTA

~

I f you make this dish during fresh basil season (July to September) take advantage of this fragrant herb, and use it in place of fresh parsley.

6 bacon slices, cut into medium dice

4 medium plum tomatoes, cut into medium dice

Salt

1 pound rigatoni *or* penne

1 cup ricotta cheese

¼ cup grated Parmesan cheese

½ cup loose-packed parsley, minced

Ground black pepper

COOKING AND SERVING Fry bacon in a medium skillet until crisp. Remove and discard all but 1 tablespoon bacon fat. Add tomatoes to the skillet; cook until heated through; cover and keep warm. Meanwhile, bring 4 quarts water to boil in a large soup kettle. Add 1 tablespoon salt and pasta; cook until tender, 10 to 12 minutes. Drain pasta and transfer to a serving bowl. Add cheeses, parsley, and bacon mixture; toss to coat. Season with ½ teaspoon pepper; serve immediately.

MAKES 4 SERVINGS

BOW TIES WITH ARUGULA, BACON, AND PARMESAN CHEESE

ome of the pasta water is reserved and mixed with a little cream to make a light but velvety sauce. Serve pasta with sliced tomato and red onion dressed with balsamic vinaigrette.

6 bacon slices, cut into ¹/₂-inch dice (6 ounces)

1 large garlic clove, minced

¹/₂ cup dry white wine

¹/₄ cup heavy cream

8 ounces arugula rinsed, stemmed, and halved crosswise

Salt

12 ounces pasta bow ties

2 ounces grated Parmesan cheese (¹/₂ cup)

Ground black pepper

COOKING Sauté bacon in a medium skillet until crisp, about 5 minutes. Remove bacon and drain on paper towels. Discard all but 2 tablespoons of the bacon drippings from the skillet. Add garlic and sauté until softened, about 3 minutes. Add wine, bring to a boil, and simmer until reduced to ¹/₄ cup, about 3 minutes. Add the cream and arugula; bring to a simmer and set aside. Meanwhile, bring 4 quarts water to boil in a large soup kettle. Add 2 teaspoons salt and the pasta; cook until just tender, about 10 minutes. Drain, reserving ¹/₂ cup of the pasta water, and return pasta to soup kettle. Stir in bacon, arugula mixture, reserved pasta water, and cheese; toss well. Season with ¹/₂ teaspoon pepper.

SERVING Transfer pasta to warm dinner plates and serve immediately.

MAKES **4** SERVINGS

FUSILLI WITH VEAL AND ARTICHOKES

M arinated artichokes are trimmed and cooked, making them usable immediately. Both the artichokes and their marinade are combined with chicken stock to make a flavorful sauce.

1 medium onion

³/₄ pound veal scallops

1 ounces Parmesan cheese

2 tablespoons olive oil

¹/₃ cup chicken stock

¹/₂ teaspoon dried thyme

2 jars marinated artichokes (6 ounces each)

Salt and ground black pepper

³/₄ pound dry fusilli *or* fettuccine

PREPARATION Peel and thinly slice the onion. Cut the veal crosswise into ¹/₂-inch strips. Grate the cheese (¹/₄ cup).

COOKING Heat oil in a large skillet. Add the veal and sauté until lightly browned, about 3 minutes; set aside. Add onions and sauté until softened, about 5 minutes. Add the chicken stock and thyme, and simmer until stock reduces slightly, about 4 minutes. Add the cooked veal, artichokes with marinade, ¹/₂ teaspoon salt, and ¹/₄ teaspoon pepper; set skillet aside. Bring 4 quarts of water to a boil in a large soup kettle. Add fusilli and 1 tablespoon salt; cook until pasta is tender, about 10 minutes; drain. Toss pasta with sauce over very low heat; adjust seasoning to taste.

SERVING Transfer the pasta to a warm serving bowl or warm plates. Sprinkle with Parmesan cheese and serve immediately.

MAKES **4** SERVINGS

RISOTTO WITH HAM AND ASPARAGUS

~

Italians serve risotto with just enough broth to coat each grain of rice. If you prefer it a bit drier, simmer the rice a minute or two longer.

4 ounces smoked ham *or* prosciutto

6 scallions

1 pound asparagus

3 tablespoons minced chervil *or* parsley

³/₄ cup white wine

6 cups chicken stock

3 tablespoons butter

1¹/₂ cups rice (preferably arborio)

Salt and ground black pepper

PREPARATION Cut ham into thin strips. Cut the scallions, including a couple of inches of the green tops, into thin slices. Trim the asparagus and cut the stalks on the diagonal into 1-inch pieces. Mince the chervil. (Recipe can be made to this point a couple of hours ahead.)

COOKING AND SERVING In a nonreactive saucepan, heat the wine and stock. Add the asparagus to the simmering stock and cook until tender, about 6 minutes. Remove with a slotted spoon and reserve. Heat the butter in a heavy, nonreactive saucepan. Sauté the ham over medium-high heat until golden, about 3 minutes. Remove ham with a slotted spoon and reserve. Add the scallions to the pan and sauté over medium-low heat for 1 minute. Add the rice and cook, stirring, until rice becomes opaque, about 1 minute. Add enough simmering stock mixture to cover the rice, about ³/₄ cup. Cook over medium heat, stirring constantly and keeping the mixture at an even, gentle simmer, until most of the liquid is absorbed, about 5 minutes. Add additional stock mixture to cover rice again and continue to cook in the same manner, adding more stock mixture as needed. When done, the rice should be tender and the remaining liquid should be thickened to a sauce. Stir in the chervil, ham, and asparagus and heat through. Season to taste with salt and pepper. Serve immediately.

MAKES **4** SERVINGS

RISOTTO WITH ARTICHOKES

I**n Italy, risotto is traditionally made with arborio rice. Arborio is short-grained and starchy, which yields the creamy texture characteristic of a good risotto. If arborio is not available, other short-grain or even long-grain rice can be substituted.**

1 clove garlic

¼ cup chopped flat-leaf parsley

¼ cup grated aged Parmesan cheese (about 1 ounce)

1 large artichoke *or* 2 smaller artichokes

Juice of ½ lemon

6 tablespoons olive oil

3 cups light chicken stock

Salt and ground black pepper

½ small onion

¾ cup arborio or other rice

⅔ cup dry white wine

2 tablespoons butter

PREPARATION Thinly slice the garlic. Chop the parsley. Grate the cheese. Cut off artichoke stem, remove tough outer leaves until only pale yellow inner leaves remain, and cut off pointy tips from tops of leaves. Cut artichoke in half, lengthwise, cut out fuzzy choke. Use a teaspoon to dig out the fuzzy fibers and wipe heart clean. Rub the artichoke at once with the lemon juice to prevent discoloration. Thinly slice each artichoke half crosswise and toss with remaining lemon juice. In a saucepan, heat 3 tablespoons of olive oil. Sauté the artichoke slices and garlic over medium heat until garlic is soft, about 3 minutes. Add ⅓ cup chicken stock, 3 tablespoons parsley, and pepper to taste. Simmer until the artichoke is just tender, about 30 minutes. Chop the onion.

COOKING Heat remaining 3 tablespoons oil in a saucepan. Cook the onion until soft. Add the rice and stir for 1 minute to coat. Stir in wine. Cook, stirring thoroughly, over medium-high heat until the wine reduces. Heat the stock and add ⅔ cup to rice. Cook, stirring continually, until all liquid is absorbed. Stir artichoke mixture into risotto. Add more stock, ⅓ cup at a time, stirring continually. Allow liquid to be thoroughly absorbed between additions. Cook until rice is creamy and grains are soft but still whole, about 20 minutes total. Stir in butter and 3 tablespoons of the cheese. Add salt and pepper to taste.

SERVING Serve risotto at once, sprinkled with remaining cheese and 1 tablespoon parsley.

MAKES 4 SERVINGS

S

affron-flavored rice lends authentic flavor to this seafood and sausage paella. A quick version of the Venetian classic, this makes a very satisfying one-dish meal.

¹/₈ teaspoon saffron threads

¹/₃ cup white wine

1 onion

1 red *or* green bell pepper

1 large clove garlic

12 littleneck clams

12 mussels

12 large shrimp

¹/₂ pound smoked sausage

3 tablespoons chopped green olives (optional)

3 tablespoon olive oil

1 cup uncooked rice

Salt and ground black pepper

¹/₈ teaspoon cayenne

1²/₃ cups fish *or* chicken stock

PREPARATION Crumble the saffron into the wine. Chop the onion and the pepper. Mince the garlic. Scrub the clams and mussels and remove beards from mussels. Peel and devein the shrimp. Cut the sausage into ¹/₂-inch thick slices. Chop the olives.

COOKING In a large frying pan or a paella pan with a lid, heat the olive oil and sauté the onion and bell pepper over medium heat until softened, about 4 minutes. Add the garlic and sauté about 1 minute. Add rice and stir to coat. Add salt and pepper and cayenne to taste. Add the stock and saffron/wine mixture and bring to a boil. Cover the pan, lower the heat, and simmer about 10 minutes. Sauté the sausage until lightly browned, about 4 minutes over medium-low heat. Drain. Push the clams into the rice. Cover the pan and simmer 5 minutes. Add the mussels and shrimp, push down, cover, and simmer another 5 minutes. Add the sausage and optional olives and simmer, covered, until rice and all shellfish are cooked and sausage is heated through, about 5 minutes.

MAKES **4** SERVINGS

W

ehani, a deep bronze-brown rice, has a

nutty aroma but it is chewy and sweet — a perfect foil for this pecan, port

wine, and carrot combination. If you cannot find wehani rice in your

market, wild rice may be substituted.

1/3 cup pecans (1 1/2 ounces)
2 cups Wehani rice (13 ounces)
2 1/2 cups chicken stock
1 small onion
1 small carrot
6 tablespoons butter
1/4 cup port wine, ruby or tawny
Salt and ground black pepper
2 tablespoons minced parsley

PREPARATION AND COOKING Adjust oven rack to middle position and heat the oven to 350°F. Put pecans in a baking dish and toast until lightly colored, about 5 minutes; coarsely chop and set aside. Bring rice and chicken stock to a boil in a medium saucepan. Cover and simmer until rice is just tender, about 45 minutes; set aside. (Can cool, cover and refrigerate overnight.)

Peel and mince onion. Peel and cut carrot into 1/4-inch dice. Heat butter in a large nonreactive skillet, add onions and carrots, and sauté until tender, about 4 minutes. Stir in port and simmer until liquid evaporates. Add rice and pecans and sauté until warm. Season with 1/4 teaspoon salt and 1/4 teaspoon pepper. Garnish with parsley; serve immediately.

MAKES 6 SERVINGS

*W*ild Pecan rice is neither wild nor tastes of pecans, but it smells nutty when cooked. Use 1 cup raw rice and 2 cups water to yield the amount of cooked Wild Pecan rice required for this recipe. Regular long-grain rice can be substituted.

2 medium onions

1 small garlic clove

1 medium green bell pepper

2 small jalapeño chiles

8 ounces canned tomatoes, drained

1/2 cup loosely packed cilantro leaves

4 scallions

1/2 pound pork tenderloin

2 eggs

3 tablespoons vegetable oil

2 cups cooked Wild Pecan rice *or* regular long-grain rice

1/2 teaspoon hot red-pepper sauce

Salt and ground black pepper

PREPARATION Peel and mince onions and garlic. Stem, seed, and cut green pepper into 1/8-inch strips. Stem, seed and mince chiles. Coarsely chop tomatoes. Mince cilantro (1/4 cup). Thinly slice scallions. Cut pork across the grain into 1/4-inch slices, then slice lengthwise into 1/4-inch wide strips. Lightly beat eggs.

COOKING Heat 2 tablespoons oil in a skillet until very hot; add the pork and sauté until lightly browned, about 4 minutes. Add onions, garlic, and peppers; sauté until tender, about 5 minutes. Push vegetables into a ring around the edge of the skillet. Add remaining oil to center of skillet and heat for 30 seconds. Pour eggs into the center and scramble until set, about 3 minutes. Immediately stir in rice, tomatoes, hot red-pepper sauce, cilantro, scallions, 1 teaspoon salt, and 1/2 teaspoon pepper. Adjust seasoning and heat until rice is warm; serve immediately.

MAKES 6 SERVINGS

T

o turn this spicy, golden-hued rice into a delicious main dish, briefly sauté either shrimp or crawfish and stir them into rice at the last minute.

½ green bell pepper
½ red bell pepper
1 jalapeño pepper
½ rib celery
2 small scallions
1 clove garlic
2 tablespoons sun-dried tomatoes
1 teaspoon chopped fresh thyme
2 cups chicken stock
1 pinch saffron
1 cup rice
¼ cup olive oil
Salt and ground black pepper

PREPARATION Stem and seed the bell peppers. Stem the jalapeño pepper. Chop the celery, scallions, bell peppers, jalapeño pepper, garlic, and sun-dried tomatoes. Mince the thyme. Put the chicken stock and saffron in a saucepan and bring to a boil. Stir in the rice and cook, covered, until tender, about 20 minutes. Remove from heat and reserve. In a skillet, heat oil over medium-high heat. Add celery, scallions, bell peppers, jalapeño, garlic, and thyme and cook until soft, about 5 minutes. Add tomatoes and cook until the tomatoes rehydrate, about 10 more minutes. Stir in rice. (Recipe can be made to this point several hours ahead.)

COOKING AND SERVING Cook rice mixture over medium heat until warmed through, about 15 minutes. Season with salt and pepper and serve.

MAKES **4** SERVINGS

SCALLOP AND BACON JAMBALAYA

≈≈

*T*he name jambalaya is believed to come from the French for ham, "jambon," and an African word for rice, "ya."

For a fiery Creole/Cajun taste, increase the quantity of cayenne pepper.

2 slices bacon *or* ham (2 ounces)

1 medium onion

1 medium garlic clove

1 small green bell pepper

1 celery stalk

2 scallions

³/₄ cup long-grain rice

1¹/₂ cups chicken stock *or* water

¹/₈ teaspoon cayenne pepper

Salt and ground black pepper

1 pound bay scallops

PREPARATION Cut the bacon into ¹/₂-inch square pieces. Chop the onion, mince the garlic, and cut the bell pepper (¹/₂ cup) and celery (¹/₄ cup) into ¹/₄-inch dice. Slice the scallions into thin rings; set aside.

COOKING AND SERVING In a 3-quart saucepan, sauté the bacon until crisp and fat is rendered, about 4 minutes. Add the onions and sauté until softened, about 3 minutes. Add the garlic and sauté for 30 seconds. Stir in the green pepper, celery, and rice, and sauté, stirring constantly, until the rice is golden and the vegetables soften slightly, about 3 minutes. Add the stock, cayennne pepper, 1 teaspoon salt, and ¹/₂ teaspoon black pepper. Bring the mixture to a boil, reduce heat, cover, and simmer until the liquid is fully absorbed, about 18 minutes. Add the scallops, cover, and simmer until they just turn opaque, about 4 minutes. Stir in the scallion rings and serve immediately.

MAKES **4** SERVINGS

*T*his pilaf is a fragrant and colorful combination where the peaches add a touch of sweetness and the toasted almonds provide the crunchy texture.

2 tablespoons slivered almonds
6 snow peas
1 lime
1½ teaspoons fresh ginger
1 scallion
1 peach
2 tablespoons butter
1 cup long-grain white rice
Salt and ground black pepper

PREPARATION Heat oven to 325°F. Spread the almonds in a shallow baking pan and toast, stirring once or twice, until lightly browned, about 5 minutes. Cool. Trim and string peas and cook in boiling, salted water until tender, about 1 minute. Drain, refresh under cold water, and drain again. Cut diagonally into ½-inch pieces. Grate zest from lime. Squeeze 2 tablespoons lime. Mince the ginger. Slice the scallion, including the green top.

COOKING AND SERVING Peel, pit, and dice the peach. Heat 1 tablespoon of the butter in a saucepan over medium heat until foamy. Add the diced peach and sauté, stirring gently until slightly softened, about 2 minutes. Remove and reserve. In the same pan, melt the remaining tablespoon of butter, add the scallions, and sauté, stirring, until softened, about 2 minutes. Add the ginger and cook 1 minute longer. Add the rice, stirring to coat with butter, and cook 1 minute. Stir in 2 cups water, lime zest, and lime juice. Bring the liquid just to a boil over high heat. Lower heat, cover, and simmer until the liquid is absorbed and the rice is tender, about 20 minutes. Stir in the toasted almonds, snow peas, and diced peach. Season to taste with salt and pepper and serve.

MAKES **4** SERVINGS

The thin, long-grain, cream-colored basmati rice is preferable to ordinary long-grain in this exotic dish. The pilaf can be simmered on top of the stove or in a 350°F oven for 15 to 18 minutes. Sliced almonds are stirred into the rice just before serving.

½ small onion
1 small garlic clove
1 small lemon
2 tablespoons sliced almonds
    (¾ ounce)
1 tablespoon olive oil
1 cup long-grain rice, preferably
    basmati (7 ounces)
1¾ cups chicken stock
¼ teaspoon tumeric
Salt and ground black pepper

PREPARATION Peel and mince onion and garlic. Grate ½ teaspoon lemon zest.

COOKING Heat a large saucepan, add almonds, and toast until golden brown, about 4 minutes. Set almonds aside. Heat oil in the saucepan. Add onion and sauté until softened, about 3 minutes. Stir in rice and garlic; sauté until rice is translucent, 1 to 2 minutes. Add chicken stock, lemon zest, turmeric, ¼ teaspoon salt, and ¼ teaspoon pepper; bring to a boil. Cover and simmer until tender, 15 to 18 minutes. Stir in almonds and serve immediately.

MAKES 6 SERVINGS

*O*riental egg noodles are available in most grocery stores and Oriental food shops. If unavailable, substitute an equal amount of dried linguine. Blanched broccoli florets, snow peas, or julienned jicama can be substituted for any of the vegetables.

Oriental Sauce
3 tablespoon soy sauce
2 tablespoons rice vinegar
2 tablespoons sugar
2 tablespoons Oriental sesame oil

Vegetable and Noodles
2 medium carrots
4 large scallions
1 large garlic clove
1 ounce ginger (1- by 1-inch piece)
1 medium red bell pepper
Salt
1 package Oriental egg noodles
  (8 ounces)
2 tablespoons vegetable oil
2 cups bean sprouts (6 ounces)
1 can sliced water chestnuts
  (8 ounces)
$1/3$ cup frozen peas ($1^1/2$ ounces)

PREPARATION *For the sauce*, mix the soy sauce, rice vinegar, sugar, and sesame oil in a small bowl; set aside. *For the vegetables and noodles*, peel and thinly slice the carrots on the diagonal. Thinly slice the scallions. Peel and mince the garlic and ginger. Stem, seed and cut the pepper lengthwise into $1/4$-inch strips.

COOKING Bring 4 quarts of water and 1 teaspoon of salt to a boil in a soup kettle. Add the noodles and cook for 2 minutes. Add the carrots and simmer until noodles and carrots are just tender, about 2 minutes longer. Drain and return noodles and carrots to the soup kettle; cover and keep warm. Heat the vegetable oil until it is hot, but not smoking, in a wok or a large skillet. Add the garlic and the ginger; stir-fry until they are fragrant, about 30 seconds. Add the scallions, bell-pepper strips, bean sprouts, drained water chestnut slices, and the peas; stir-fry until the vegetables soften slightly, about 2 minutes. Add the vegetables to the soup kettle along with the oriental sauce. Toss over high heat until mixture is hot, making sure the noodles are coated with the sauce. Serve immediately.

MAKES 4 SERVINGS

Y*ou can mix up this basic popover batter in just a few minutes. Some say it is better prepared in advanced. The secret to puffy, golden-domed popovers is to avoid overbeating.*

1 cup unbleached white flour (5 ounces)

1/4 teaspoon salt

1 cup milk

1 tablespoon melted butter

2 eggs

PREPARATION Heat oven to 350°F. Generously oil popover pans, cups, or tins and preheat them. Beat all ingredients together until just smooth, being careful not to overbeat. Batter should be the consistency of heavy cream. Fill prepared pans 1/2 to 2/3 full.

COOKING Bake in preheated oven 15 minutes. Lower temperature to 350°F without opening oven door and bake until popovers are firm and golden brown, 15 to 20 minutes more. Remove from oven and make slits in the bottom to release the steam.

SERVING Serve immediately.

VARIATIONS For cheddar cheese popovers, add 3 ounces grated sharp cheddar cheese to completed popover batter and bake as directed above. Or, for Parmesan-basil popovers, stir 1 1/2 ounces coarse-grated Parmesan cheese and 1 tablespoon minced fresh basil into completed popover batter and bake as directed above.

MAKES ❽ POPOVERS

BLUEBERRY CORN MUFFINS

✃

*T*hese blueberry-studded muffins turn out dense and moist on the inside, and rough and pebbly on the outside.

1 cup white cornmeal

2 cups all-purpose flour

1/3 cup sugar

4 teaspoons baking powder

1/2 teaspoon salt

2 eggs, beaten

2 cups milk

4 tablespoons unsalted butter, melted

3/4 cup fresh blueberries

PREPARATION Heat oven to 425°F. Butter and flour 2-inch muffin tins. In a mixing bowl, sift together cornmeal, flour, sugar, baking powder, and salt. Make a well in center. In another bowl, beat together eggs and milk. Pour egg mixture and melted butter into well and stir just enough to combine. Fold in blueberries. Fill prepared muffin tins 2/3 full.

COOKING Bake in preheated oven until muffins test done, 15 to 20 minutes. Cool on rack.

MAKES **1** DOZEN MUFFINS

BLUE AND YELLOW CORNSTICKS AND MUFFINS

*S*erving blue and yellow cornmeal muffins and sticks adds variety to the bread basket. However, the cornmeals are interchangeable in the recipe. The tenderness of the muffins result from the relatively large quantities of shortening and cream.

4 tablespoons butter

½ small red onion

2 tablespoons vegetable shortening

1 egg

⅔ cup blue or yellow cornmeal

⅓ cup all-purpose flour

2 tablespoons sugar

1½ teaspoons baking powder

½ teaspoon salt

¼ teaspoon cayenne pepper

1 cup heavy cream

PREPARATION AND COOKING Adjust oven rack to low position and heat oven to 425°F. Generously coat 12 muffin tins (with 2½-inch diameter cups) or 2 cornstick pans (with seven 5½- by 1½-inch molds) with 2 tablespoons of the butter. Peel and mince 2 tablespoons of onion. Heat shortening and remaining butter in a small skillet, add the onion, and sauté over medium heat until softened, about 2 minutes. Transfer onion mixture to a bowl and cool slightly. Separate the egg and add the yolk to the bowl. Stir in cornmeal, flour, sugar, baking powder, salt, and cayenne pepper. Stir in the cream. Whip the egg white to soft peaks and fold it into the batter. Spoon the batter into the cups or molds. Bake muffins or cornsticks until they are golden, about 15 to 20 minutes. Serve them warm.

MAKES **1** DOZEN MUFFINS OR CORNSTICKS

Corn Muffins with Spiced Ham

Corn and ham complement each other in these spicy muffins, which can be served piping hot from the oven or cooled to room temperature.

¾ cup frozen corn kernels

1½ ounces tasso *or* other spicy ham

¼ red bell pepper

1½ teaspoons minced fresh
    coriander (optional)

¾ cup sour cream

2 tablespoons oil

2 eggs

¾ cup yellow cornmeal

3 tablespoons flour

2¼ teaspoons baking powder

¼ teaspoon cayenne pepper

½ teaspoon salt

2 teaspoons sugar

PREPARATION Heat oven to 400°F. Thaw corn. Butter muffin tins. Dice the ham. Chop the red bell pepper. Mince the coriander. In a bowl, combine the sour cream, oil, corn, ham, bell pepper, and coriander. Lightly beat eggs and add to mixture. In a separate bowl, mix together the cornmeal, flour, baking powder, cayenne, salt, and sugar. Add dry ingredients to the sour cream mixture and stir to combine. Pour into prepared muffin tins and bake in preheated oven until golden brown, about 20 minutes. Cool for about 5 minutes in the tin.

SERVING Serve warm, or cool the muffins to room temperature.

MAKES ❶ DOZEN MUFFINS

Saffron Cornbread

~

affron, which ranks as the most costly sea-soning in the world, adds a warm and pungent flavor and a characteristic golden yellow color to many traditional dishes.

1 cup unbleached flour

2 cups stone-ground cornmeal

1½ teaspoons salt

4 teaspoons baking powder

1 teaspoon baking soda

2 tablespoons sugar

½ teaspoon (scant) saffron, toasted in 350°F oven 3 minutes and then powdered

2 cups buttermilk

1½ cups grated sharp Wisconsin Asiago cheese *or* 2 cups grated mild Wisconsin Asiago cheese *or* 1 cup grated Parmesan cheese

2 large eggs

8 tablespoons unsalted butter, melted

PREPARATION Heat oven to 400°F. Generously butter a 13- by 9-by 2-inch baking pan. In a large bowl, combine flour, cornmeal, salt, baking powder, soda, and sugar. Steep saffron in buttermilk for 10 minutes. Put pan in preheated oven to heat for 5 minutes. In another bowl, whisk together saffron/buttermilk, cheese, eggs, and melted butter. Gently fold this mixture into dry ingredients, being careful not to overmix.

COOKING Pour into hot, buttered pan and bake in preheated oven until golden and set, 20 to 25 minutes.

MAKES 24 TWO-INCH SQUARES

*E*veryone loves the smell and taste of freshly baked homemade biscuits. These can be made in less time than it takes to buy a loaf of store-bought bread.

2 tablespoons chopped fresh
    tarragon *or* other herb such as
    parsley or chives

³/₄ pound potatoes (about 2)

3 cups flour

2 tablespoons plus 2 teaspoons
    baking powder

2 tablespoons sugar

Salt and ground black pepper

6 ounces butter

1 to 1¹/₄ cups milk

PREPARATION Chop the tarragon. Peel the potatoes and cut into rough, ¹/₂-inch dice. Put the potatoes in a saucepan with cold, salted water to cover. Bring to a boil and cook until potatoes are tender, about 10 minutes. Drain. Meanwhile, sift together the flour, baking powder, sugar, 1¹/₂ teaspoons salt, and ¹/₄ teaspoon pepper. Mash the potatoes while still hot. Beat in the butter and 1 cup milk until smooth. Stir the potato mixture, the flour mixture, and the tarragon just until a soft dough forms and mixture cleans sides of bowl. Add up to ¹/₄ cup milk if needed. Turn dough onto a lightly floured work surface and knead until smooth, about 1 minute. Roll or pat into ¹/₂-inch thickness and cut with a 1¹/₂-inch biscuit cutter. (Recipe can be made to this point 1 hour ahead.)

COOKING AND SERVING Heat oven to 425°F. Put biscuits on an unbuttered baking sheet and bake in preheated oven until golden brown, about 12 minutes. Serve warm.

MAKES 20 BISCUITS

Y

ou can vary the flavor of these biscuits with your choice of cheese and herbs. Try Havarti cheese and dill, Monterey Jack and coriander, or mozzarella and rosemary.

3 ounces sharp cheddar cheese

4 ounces unsalted butter, chilled, cut in 8 pieces

1½ cups all-purpose flour

1½ teaspoons baking powder

½ teaspoon salt

1 tablespoon minced fresh basil leaves

¼ cup milk

PREPARATION AND COOKING Heat oven to 425°F. In a food processor, shred cheese. Distribute pieces of butter around bowl of processor and pulse just to combine. Add flour, baking powder, salt, and basil and pulse just until butter is incorporated into dry ingredients and mixture resembles large crumbs. Add milk and pulse until dough begins to clump together. Turn dough out onto a lightly floured work surface, knead 2 or 3 times to form a ball, and pat or roll to ³/₄-inch thickness. Cut dough into rounds, using a floured 1½- or 2-inch biscuit cutter. Put biscuits on a baking sheet and bake until golden.

MAKES **2** DOZEN BISCUITS

SEAFOOD

Broiled Oysters
with Wine Sauce
84

Sausages and
Oysters
85

Oysters in
Champagne Sauce
86

Baked Oysters with
Chile-Coriander
Pesto
87

Mussels with
Tomato and Pernod
Butter
88

Scallops in
White Wine
89

Cajun Shrimp
Sandwich
90

Shrimp with Tuna
Fish Sauce
91

Shrimp Rockefeller
92

Grilled Shrimp with
Cilantro
93

Skewered Shrimp
and Scallions
94

Tuna Steaks Stuffed
with Smoked Gouda
95

Grouper en
Escabeche
96

Island Escabeche
97

Grilled Salmon with
Chinese Mustard
and Leeks
98

Salmon in
Court Bouillon
99

Sizzled Salmon with
Lime Butter
101

Halibut with
Smoked Salmon and
Dill Butter
102

Poached Halibut
with Cream Sauce
103

Red Snapper with
Sweet and Hot
Peppers
104

Fish Steaks with
Thyme
105

Swordfish with
Tomatoes and Basil
106

Grilled Swordfish
with Beurre Blanc
107

Grilled Swordfish
Sandwich
109

Tuna Steaks with
Caper Mayonnaise
110

Grilled Tuna with
Basil and Red
Peppers
111

BROILED OYSTERS WITH SHALLOT WINE SAUCE

❧

You can make the sauce ahead of time and hold it over a pan of hot water up to one hour.

5 shallots

24 oysters

1¹/₂ cup white wine

¹/₄ pound butter

1 teaspoon lemon juice

Salt and ground black pepper

PREPARATION Mince the shallots. Shuck the oysters, reserving juices and the deep halves of the shells. In a skillet, barely cook the oysters in their juices over low heat, about 15 seconds. In a saucepan, combine the oyster liquid, wine, and shallots. Reduce to 1 tablespoon over medium high heat, about 10 minutes. (Recipe can be made to this point a few hours ahead.)

COOKING AND SERVING Heat the broiler. Set wine mixture over the lowest possible heat and whisk in the butter about a tablespoon at a time, adding a new piece as each one is incorporated. Butter should not melt completely but soften to form a creamy sauce. Add reduced oyster juice and season to taste with lemon juice and salt and pepper. Spoon a little sauce into each oyster shell, top with an oyster, and nap with a bit more sauce. Put under preheated broiler until browned, about 1 minute.

MAKES ❹ SERVINGS

Odd though this may sound, sausages and oysters are an old and venerable combination in French cuisine. Larger varieties of oysters are better than small ones for this treatment, as they are easier to handle on a hot grill when roasted. Fried onions and sweet peppers, along with some Italian bread, are the best accompaniments.

24 oysters

1 pound hot *or* sweet Italian
sausages

PREPARATION Scrub the oysters.

COOKING Heat the grill. Cook the sausages over a medium-hot bed of coals, turning frequently, until skin is crisp and sausages are just cooked through, about 10 minutes. About 3 minutes before sausages are done, put the oysters on the grill, deep shell down, and cook until they open, about 3 minutes. Be careful when handling the oysters; the shells sometimes pop.

MAKES **4** SERVINGS

*T*he microwave oven is ideal for this simple and elegant classic. You can prepare the oysters and sauce ahead in the microwave, and then broil for a minute or two just before serving.

24 oysters

Champagne Sauce
1½ tablespoons unsalted butter
1½ tablespoons flour
½ cup oyster juice, from above
½ cup Champagne *or* other dry
  sparkling wine
¼ teaspoon ground celery seed
Freshly ground white pepper

2 cups coarse *or* rock salt for the
  broiler pan

PREPARATION *To open the oysters*, scrub well to remove sand and barnacles. In a 14- by 11- by 2-inch microwaveable baking dish, stand oysters on their sides. Cover tightly with plastic wrap and microwave on high until oysters just begin to open, about 9 minutes. Make a slit in the plastic wrap to allow steam to escape. Remove plastic. Open oysters over a bowl to catch juices. Loosen oysters from shells. Reserve deep shell halves and oysters; discard shallow halves. Strain liquid from bowl and cooking dish through a sieve lined with moistened cheesecloth or a coffee filter. Measure ½ cup of the strained cooking liquid and reserve.

For the Champagne Sauce, melt the butter in a 1-quart glass or ceramic measure or bowl, uncovered, on high for 2 minutes. Whisk in flour and cook, uncovered, on high for 2 minutes. Stir in ½ cup reserved oyster juices and Champagne and cook, uncovered, on high, stirring twice during cooking, for 4 minutes or until thickened. Recipe can be made to this point a few hours ahead.

COOKING AND SERVING Heat the broiler with rack set at its highest level. Stir celery seed and white pepper to taste into the sauce. Spread 2 cups of coarse or rock salt in the bottom of a broiler pan to steady oysters. Nestle reserved shells into salt. Put each oyster in a shell and thoroughly coat the tops with sauce. Put under preheated broiler until just golden, about 2 minutes.

MAKES 4 FIRST-COURSE SERVINGS

BAKED OYSTERS WITH CHILE-CORIANDER PESTO

The Southwest flavors in this pesto make a bright and tangy topping for the baked oysters.

3 dark green, spicy chiles, such as pasillas *or* Italian frying peppers

2 small, hot red peppers, such as tiger chiles

3 cloves garlic

¼ cup pine nuts

3 tablespoons hard goat cheese *or* Romano cheese plus more for sprinkling

3 tablespoons grated Parmesan cheese

¼ cup coriander leaves

Pinch nutmeg

Salt and ground black pepper

¾ cup vegetable oil

16 to 20 oysters on the half shell

Lemon *or* lime wedges for garnish

PREPARATION Roast chiles or peppers over a gas flame, charcoal grill, or under broiler until skin is blackened. Cool, and then remove skin, stems, seeds, and ribs. Put chiles, garlic, pine nuts, and cheeses in a food processor or blender and puree to a fine paste. Add coriander, nutmeg, and salt and pepper to taste. With motor running, slowly pour in oil. Refrigerate, covered, until ready to use.

COOKING Heat oven to 400°F. Put oysters on a baking sheet and spoon 1 teaspoon pesto over each oyster. Bake in preheated oven for 6 minutes. Remove oysters from oven. Heat broiler. Sprinkle oysters with goat cheese or Romano cheese. Return them to oven or broiler until they brown, 1 to 2 minutes. Remove and serve with lemon or lime wedges.

MAKES **4** APPETIZER SERVINGS

A hint of licorice in the Pernod-flavored tomato butter gives an interesting touch to these broiled mussels.

3 pounds mussels

3 shallots

²/₃ cup white wine

1 small bay leaf

Tomato and Pernod Butter

1 shallot

2 cloves garlic

2 teaspoons chopped parsley

³/₄ pound softened butter

1 tablespoon tomato paste

2 tablespoons Pernod

3 tablespoons bread crumbs

1 teaspoon *herbes de Provence* or a
    mixture of sage, rosemary, and
    thyme

Salt and ground black pepper

MAKES **4** SERVINGS

PREPARATION Scrub and debeard the mussels. Chop the shallots. Put the wine, shallots, and bay leaf in a large pot, bring to a boil over high heat, and cook for 1 minute. Add the mussels and cook, covered, until mussels just open, about 4 more minutes. Remove from heat. When mussels are cool enough to handle, remove them from their shells. Clean out 1 half of each shell and put a mussel inside. Put on a baking sheet and set aside.

For the Tomato and Pernod Butter, mince the shallot and garlic. Chop the parsley. Combine all ingredients for the butter in the bowl of a food processor, season to taste with salt and pepper, and process until smooth. Cover each mussel with Tomato and Pernod Butter. Refrigerate until butter is firm.

COOKING AND SERVING Heat the broiler. Brown mussels under preheated broiler, about 2 minutes.

SCALLOPS IN WHITE WINE, SHALLOTS, AND HERBS

❧

Although this recipe calls for pink scallops, indigenous to the Northwest, you can use mussels as a good alternative.

1 pound unshelled pink scallops *or*
    mussels
1 shallot
¼ cup white wine
4 tablespoons butter
Pinch thyme
1 broken bay leaf
Ground black pepper

PREPARATION Scrub scallops or mussels clean. Chop the shallot.
COOKING Bring the wine, butter, shallot, thyme, bay leaf, and pepper to a boil. Add the shellfish, cover tightly, and steam over low heat until scallops are just cooked through and begin to fall from their shells, 2 to 3 minutes. If using mussels, cook just until they open, about 5 to 10 minutes. Discard bay leaf.
SERVING Serve in broth in warm bowls.

MAKES **4** SERVINGS

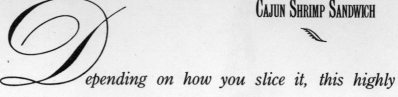

epending on how you slice it, this highly

spiced, Cajun-flavored sandwich can be an appetizer or a whole meal.

½ rib celery

½ green pepper

4 scallions

1 tomato

¾ pound shrimp

4 grinder rolls

4 tablespoons butter

½ teaspoon red-pepper flakes

½ teaspoon dried oregano

Salt and gound black pepper

1 tablespoon Madeira

Hot red-pepper sauce

PREPARATION Chop the celery, green pepper, and scallions. Peel and chop the tomato. Shell the shrimp.

COOKING Warm the rolls. In a skillet, heat the butter. Sauté the celery, green pepper, and scallions until soft, about 3 minutes. Stir in the tomato, red-pepper flakes, oregano, salt and pepper, and shrimp. Cook until shrimp are pink and cooked through, 2 to 3 minutes. Stir in Madeira and cook over high heat, about 30 seconds. Adjust seasonings.

SERVING Spoon shrimp mixture into warm rolls and serve with hot red-pepper sauce on the side.

MAKES **4** SERVINGS

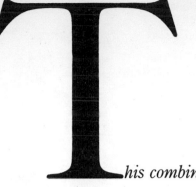

This combination of shrimp and tuna makes a great party dish. Imported, canned Italian tuna fish will give this dip a particularly assertive taste.

18 large shrimp (about 1 pound)
1 lemon
1 can chunk light tuna, packed in olive oil (3 ounces)
3 tablespoons mayonnaise
1 tablespoon stemmed, minced parsley leaves
1 tablespoon drained capers

PREPARATION AND COOKING Shell and devein the shrimp, leaving the tails intact. Put 6 cups of water into a large saucepan. Squeeze in the juice of half the lemon and bring to a boil. Drop the shrimp into the boiling water, turn heat to low, and cook until pink, about 1 minute. Remove saucepan from heat, cool shrimp in the poaching liquid, then drain and set them aside. Put tuna and mayonnaise in the workbowl of a food processor fitted with the metal blade. Squeeze in juice from remaining lemon and puree. Pulse in the parsley. (Can cover and refrigerate the shrimp and sauce overnight.)

SERVING Put tuna sauce in a dish and sprinkle with capers. Arrange shrimp on a platter in an attractive pattern around the dish of sauce. Serve at room temperature.

MAKES 18 PIECES

his shrimp version of the traditional Oysters Rockefeller is especially light and low in fat.

Vegetable-oil spray

1/2 onion, diced

6 cups chopped spinach

1/2 teaspoon Pernod

3/4 pound shrimp, peeled

2 tablespoons unsalted, fat-free chicken stock

1 1/2 teaspoons minced fresh herbs, such as basil, thyme, sage, parsley or chives or a mixture *or* 1/2 teaspoon dried

1/4 cup low-fat milk

1 1/2 teaspoons arrowroot, dissolved in 2 tablespoons Chablis

Salt (optional)

1/2 ounce shredded Jarlsberg cheese

COOKING AND SERVING Lightly coat a skillet with vegetable-oil spray. Sauté onion over medium heat until soft, about 3 minutes. Stir in spinach and Pernod. Simmer, tossing, until spinach just wilts, about 5 minutes. Remove from heat and set aside. In a covered steamer set over boiling water, steam shrimp 3 minutes. Remove from heat and set aside. Heat broiler. *For the sauce*, bring chicken stock and herbs to a simmer in a saucepan. Whisk in milk and arrowroot/wine mixture. Cook until sauce is thickened. Do not boil. Season to taste. Put spinach on an ovenproof dish. Arrange shrimp on spinach, top with sauce, and sprinkle on cheese. Put under preheated broiler until cheese melts, just a few seconds. Serve immediately.

MAKES **4** SERVINGS

GRILLED SHRIMP WITH CILANTRO

This is a party-size recipe for Mexican-fla-vored shrimp, which can be served as an appetizer or as part of a buffet.

1 jalapeño pepper
1 large tomato
1 large bunch cilantro (1 cup shredded leaves)
4 pounds jumbo shrimp
Salt and white pepper
1¼ pounds butter
2 limes

PREPARATION Char the jalapeño over a gas flame, under the broiler, or on the grill until skin is blackened. Peel, seed, and mince. Peel, seed, and chop the tomato and season to taste with salt and pepper. Peel and devein shrimp.

COOKING Heat grill or broiler. Melt the butter. Add jalapeño and ¼ cup shredded cilantro, squeeze in juice from the limes, and season with salt and pepper. Brush shrimp with some of the melted mixture and season with salt and pepper. Grill or broil shrimp until it just tests done, about 2 minutes total.

SERVING Put remaining butter sauce on each plate and top with about 5 shrimp and a dollop of tomato in the center.

MAKES **12** SERVINGS

SKEWERED SHRIMP AND SCALLIONS

*S*hrimp *of any size retain more of their natu-ral flavor and juiciness if cooked in the shell, whether boiled, broiled, or grilled. The shells are inedible, but true aficionados chew on them like rib bones to extract the last bit of flavor.*

Marinade

1 clove garlic

1 tablespoon minced fresh
    marjoram *or* 1 teaspoon dried

1 cup olive oil

Salt and ground black pepper

16 jumbo shrimp (about 1³/₄
    pounds)

2 large bunches scallions

2 zucchini (each about 5 inches
    long)

PREPARATION *For the marinade,* crush the garlic to a paste. Combine all marinade ingredients.

Remove the legs and slit the shrimp shells down the back. Without removing the shells, devein shrimp and slice them open about ¹/₂-inch. Cut the green tops off scallions and cut the zucchini into approximately 1 inch pieces. Marinate shrimp and vegetables at room temperature for about an hour or up to overnight in the refrigerator. Alternately thread the shrimp and scallion bulbs onto the same skewers. Put the zucchini pieces on separate skewers.

COOKING Heat the grill. Brush the skewered ingredients with marinade and grill over a medium-low bed of coals, turning once, until just cooked through, about 8 minutes in all for the shrimp and scallions, about 10 minutes for the zucchini.

MAKES **4** SERVINGS

TUNA STEAKS STUFFED WITH SAGE AND SMOKED GOUDA

❧

*U*sing the optional sage twigs on the fire gives the tuna a light, smoky-sage taste that intensifies the flavor of the sage stuffing. If tuna is not available, you can substitute swordfish.

1 handful woody sage twigs
   (optional)

2 tablespoons unsalted butter

3 tablespoons olive oil

6 sage sprigs, tied together to form
   a "brush"

Salt and ground black pepper

4 six- to eight-ounce tuna steaks,
   each about 1-inch thick

2 teaspoons minced fresh sage
   leaves

2 ounces smoked Gouda, cut into
   thin strips

PREPARATION Soak optional sage twigs in water to cover for 15 minutes. Heat grill. In a small saucepan, heat butter, olive oil, and sage sprig brush (standing up) over low heat just until butter is melted. Cut a deep but small incision in the side of each fish steak with a sharp knife and carefully move knife blade back and forth to form a pocket. Lightly salt and pepper exterior of fish. Toss minced sage with Gouda and stuff sage and cheese into each pocket.

COOKING Drain optional sage twigs and sprinkle over coals in preheated grill. Using sage-sprig brush, coat each side of fish with some butter/oil mixture. Grill until fish is just cooked through and cheese is melted, brushing often with butter/oil mixture, about 4 minutes per side. Serve immediately with any remaining butter/oil mixture drizzled over fish.

MAKES 4 SERVINGS

GROUPER EN ESCABECHE

ass, salmon, or almost any fish can be substituted for the grouper. This dish is often confused with seviche.

1 green bell pepper
1 red bell pepper
2 carrots
1 large onion
½ teaspoon chopped fresh ginger
6 tomatoes
⅓ cup olive oil
½ teaspoon red-pepper flakes
1 bay leaf
¼ teaspoon black peppercorns
¼ teaspoon mace
1½ teaspoons allspice
Salt and ground black pepper
½ cup red-wine vinegar
1½ pounds grouper fillets

PREPARATION Core and seed bell peppers. Cut peppers, carrots, and onion into thin julienne strips. Chop ginger. Core, peel, and seed tomatoes and puree in a food processor until smooth. Heat 3 tablespoons of the oil in a large frying pan over high heat. Add the bell peppers, carrots, onion, ginger, red-pepper flakes, bay leaf, peppercorns, mace, allspice, and salt to taste and sauté about 5 minutes. Add ½ cup water, pureed tomatoes, and vinegar and simmer 15 minutes. Strain, reserving both vegetable mixture and juice. (Recipe can be made to this point several hours ahead.)

COOKING Heat the oven to 375°F. Heat remaining ¼ cup of oil in a large frying pan. Sprinkle the fish with salt and pepper and sauté over high heat, turning once, until crisp, about 6 minutes. Transfer the fish to a shallow baking dish. Cover with the vegetable mixture and enough of the reserved juices to come halfway up the fish. Bake in preheated oven until fish is just cooked through, about 7 minutes.

MAKES 4 SERVINGS

T*here are many different versions of escabeche. Here the fish fillets are doused in a tart sauce and served either hot or cooled at room temperature.*

Sauce
2 green bell peppers
2 onions
1 tablespoon chopped fresh ginger
2 bay leaves
12 whole black peppercorns
1/8 teaspoon mace
1/8 teaspoon allspice
Salt
3 tablespoons vinegar
2 tablespoons olive oil

1 1/2 pounds flounder *or* sole fillets
Flour for dredging
1/2 cup olive oil

PREPARATION *For the sauce*, cut bell peppers and onions into thin slices. Peel and chop the ginger. In a nonreactive saucepan, mix together the bell peppers, onions, ginger, bay leaves, peppercorns, mace, allspice, 1 teaspoon salt, and 1/2 cup water. Cover, bring to a simmer, and cook, stirring occasionally, for 30 minutes. Add the vinegar and 2 tablespoons of the olive oil and continue simmering, covered, for an additional 2 minutes. Remove bay leaves and peppercorns from the sauce. (Sauce can be made a day ahead.)

COOKING AND SERVING Reheat sauce if necessary. Dip the fillets in water and coat lightly in flour. In a skillet, heat remaining 1/2 cup of olive oil over high heat. Add fish, reduce heat to medium, and cook, turning once, until brown, about 4 minutes total. Pour the hot sauce over the fish fillets and serve warm or let cool to room temperature.

MAKES 6 APPETIZERS OR 4 MAIN-COURSE SERVINGS

T

✗

he salmon's accompanying mild, flavorful leeks are lightly brushed with olive oil and briefly grilled.

2 leeks, white and light green part only

2 one-inch thick salmon steaks, (8 to 10 ounces each)

Olive oil for brushing

Salt and ground black pepper

2 tablespoons sugar

2 tablespoons dry mustard

PREPARATION Heat grill. Slice leeks lengthwise to base without going through it. Clean leeks thoroughly. In a pot of boiling salted water, blanch leeks until tender, about $1^1/_2$ minutes. Plunge them into cold water immediately to stop cooking. Cut each salmon steak in half and remove the backbone. Brush fish generously with olive oil, season with salt and pepper, and set aside. In a small bowl, mix sugar with dry mustard and add enough warm water (about 3 tablespoons) to make mixture the consistency of heavy cream.

COOKING Put salmon on grill and brush with mustard sauce. Cut leeks through their bases and put them on grill. Brush leeks lightly with olive oil and cook until lightly browned. Remove leeks from grill, sprinkle with salt and pepper, and set aside. Cook salmon, brushing occasionally with mustard sauce, until just done but still rosy-colored at the center, about 8 minutes. Serve on warm plates.

MAKES 4 SERVINGS

This beautiful dish maintains the special
flavor and appealing rosy color of the salmon at its very best.

3 cups Court Bouillon (recipe
    follows)
1/2 teaspoon sugar

Herb Butter
1 small shallot
1 1/2 tablespoons chopped fresh
    chervil *or* parsley
1 1/2 teaspoons chopped chives
1/4 teaspoon lemon zest
4 tablespoons softened butter
Salt and ground black pepper

4 one-inch thick pieces of skinned
    salmon fillet (about 4 ounces
    each)

PREPARATION Make the court bouillon, combining the sugar with all other ingredients before simmering. *For the butter*, dice the shallot. Chop the chervil. Chop chives. Grate zest from lemon. In a bowl, combine butter with the herbs, lemon zest, and salt and pepper to taste. Set aside.

COOKING AND SERVING Reheat the bouillon. Poach the salmon in the bouillon until fish is just cooked through, about 5 minutes. Transfer the salmon to warm soup plates and top with a dollop of Herb Butter. Remove parsley and thyme and pour hot bouillon over all.

MAKES 4 SERVINGS

*T*his delicate stock is used primarily for cooking fish, but it can also be used in vegetable and meat dishes. It can be made a day ahead.

1 small carrot
1 small rib celery
1/2 yellow onion
3 sprigs fresh *or* dried thyme
1 large sprig parsley
3 cups water
1/2 cup white wine
Salt

PREPARATION Peel carrot and cut into thin slices. Cut celery and onion into thin slices. In a nonreactive pot, combine the vegetables, herbs, water, wine, and 1 1/2 teaspoons salt. Bring to a simmer and cook, covered, for 20 minutes.

MAKES 3 CUPS

SIZZLED SALMON WITH LIME BUTTER

This salmon is cooked right on the serving plates. If you do not have ovenproof dinner plates, you can cook the salmon in a shallow baking dish.

1 pound fresh salmon fillet
2 shallots
1 lime
4 tablespoons butter

PREPARATION Holding a very sharp knife so that the blade is almost parallel to the work surface, cut salmon into paper-thin slices. Chop the shallots. Grate zest from the lime.

COOKING Heat oven to 350°F. Put four ovenproof dinner plates in preheated oven until very hot, about 3 minutes. Meanwhile, sauté shallot in butter until slightly brown. Squeeze in lime juice and sprinkle in zest. Shake pan to combine. When butter sizzles, coat each plate with about 1/2 tablespoon of the butter and immediately put fish on the hot plates. Pour remaining butter over salmon and serve immediately.

MAKES **4** SERVINGS

HALIBUT WITH SMOKED SALMON AND DILL BUTTER

℞

Smoked salmon is an uncommon ingredient in a compound butter. This butter also is delicious on grilled swordfish.

Smoked Salmon and Dill Butter
1/2 cup softened unsalted butter
1/8 cup firmly packed stemmed dill
    sprigs
1 ounce smoked salmon
Ground black pepper

1 1/2 to 2 pounds halibut steaks (four
    1-inch thick steaks)
Salt and ground black pepper

PREPARATION *For the salmon and dill butter,* cream the butter in a bowl, or put butter in the workbowl of a food processor fitted with the metal blade and process until smooth. Mince the dill and stir it thoroughly into the butter. Coarsely chop the smoked salmon and stir or process into the butter. Stir in 1/4 teaspoon pepper and adjust seasoning to taste. (Can wrap in plastic and refrigerate, or freeze up to 1 month.)

COOKING AND SERVING Bring compound butter to room temperature. Adjust the oven rack to lowest position and heat oven to 400°F. Arrange the halibut steaks in a shallow baking dish just large enough to hold all the fish pieces in a single layer. Add enough water to reach halfway up the side of each of the fish steaks. Sprinkle fish with salt and pepper and bake until done, 8 to 10 minutes. Transfer fish to serving plates. Put a tablespoon of the salmon and dill butter on top of each portion and serve immediately.

MAKES **4** SERVINGS

*H*alibut is the fish of choice for this dish, but any lean, white-fleshed fish such as mahimahi, monkfish, cod, or tilefish can all be substituted.

3 medium carrots

2 medium celery stalks

1 small onion

1½ pounds halibut (four 1-inch thick steaks)

2 teaspoons fresh thyme leaves *or* ¾ teaspoon dried

Salt and ground black pepper

1 bay leaf

½ cup dry white wine

½ cup clam juice

¼ cup heavy cream

PREPARATION Peel and diagonally slice the carrots, ⅛ inch thick. Slice the celery diagonally, ⅛ inch thick. Peel and coarsely chop the onion.

COOKING Put the fish, celery, carrots, onion, thyme, 1 teaspoon salt, ¼ teaspoon pepper, and bay leaf in a deep, nonreactive skillet large enough to hold the fish in one layer. Add the wine and clam juice. Bring liquid to a boil and simmer, partially covered, 5 minutes. Simmer until fish is just cooked, about 4 minutes longer.

SERVING Transfer fish to warm dinner plates; cover plates and keep warm. Increase heat to high and reduce the poaching liquid to ⅓ cup, about 5 minutes. Whisk in the cream and bring to a boil. Adjust seasoning to taste. Spoon the sauce and vegetables onto plates around the warm fish and serve immediately.

MAKES **4** SERVINGS

RED SNAPPER WITH SWEET AND HOT PEPPERS

❧

When peeling, seeding, and slicing hot peppers, remember not to rub the eye, mouth, or sensitive areas around the nose. Rubber gloves are a good way to keep capsaicin, the substance in the ribs of the peppers, from causing a burning sensation.

1½ to 2 pounds red snapper fillets
(about 4 small fillets)
4 medium jalapeño peppers
½ medium red bell pepper
½ medium yellow bell pepper
1 medium garlic clove
⅓ cup flour
Salt and ground black pepper
6 tablespoons butter
3 tablespoons sherry wine vinegar
¾ cup chicken stock

COOKING AND SERVING Remove the thin line of bones from the wide end of each fillet. Core, seed, and cut all the peppers into ¼-inch-thick strips. Peel and mince the garlic. Put the flour, ½ teaspoon salt, and ¼ teaspoon pepper on a flat dish. Dredge each side of the fillets in the flour mixture. Heat 4 tablespoons of the butter in a medium skillet. Add peppers and sauté, until softened, about 2 minutes. Transfer the peppers to a plate with a slotted spoon. Turn heat to medium-high, add the fish, skin side up, and sauté until just done, about 5 minutes. Turn fish and sauté on the skin side for 1 minute. Transfer fish to warm serving plates. Add the garlic, peppers, vinegar, and stock to the skillet. Bring the liquid to a boil and simmer until liquid reduces to ½ cup, about 3 minutes. Remove pan from heat and stir in remaining 2 tablespoons butter. Spoon sauce over fish and serve immediately.

MAKES **4** SERVINGS

Fish Steaks with Thyme

*T*his recipe could be used equally well with mako shark, swordfish, or tuna steaks. If you want a smoky flavor, throw a large bunch of thyme twigs onto the coals when grilling steaks, cover, and let flavor infuse for about 2 minutes. Or you could smoke with grapevine cuttings or mild wood chips and rub dried thyme into the steaks before grilling.

1¼ pounds mako shark, swordfish, *or* tuna steaks (about 1½ inches thick)

3 tablespoons oil

1 teaspoon dried thyme leaves (optional)

Salt and ground black pepper

2 tablespoons butter

PREPARATION Rub the fish steaks with the oil, thyme leaves (unless you're smoking with thyme twigs), and ½ teaspoon pepper and marinate at room temperature for about ½ hour before grilling.

COOKING AND SERVING Heat the grill. Melt the butter. Sprinkle the fish steaks with salt and set them on the grill at least 6 inches from the coals. Cook about 5 minutes in all, turning and switching position on the grill to make a crosshatch pattern. Remove from grill and brush with butter.

MAKES 4 SERVINGS

SWORDFISH WITH TOMATOES AND BASIL

❧

Saucing a grilled swordfish steak with a riotous tricolored tomato salad may seem slightly extravagant. But the salad marries perfectly with grilled swordfish and the acidity of the tomatoes, in combination with an undertone of garlic and the slight sweetness of the vinegar, complements the fish dramatically.

2 pounds assorted tomatoes (cherry or beefsteak tomatoes, yellow plum tomatoes, *and/or* tomatillos)

3 tablespoons balsamic vinegar

6 tablespoons olive oil

2 medium garlic cloves

½ cup firmly packed stemmed basil leaves

Salt and ground black pepper

1½ to 2 pounds swordfish steaks (four 1-inch thick steaks)

PREPARATION Rinse and cut tomatoes into 1-inch chunks (5 cups). Put the tomatoes, balsamic vinegar, and 3 tablespoons of the olive oil in a medium bowl and marinate at room temperature for 30 minutes. (Can marinate up to 2 hours.)

COOKING Heat the grill. Mince the garlic and the basil and stir into the tomatoes with ½ teaspoon salt and ¼ teaspoon pepper. With a small, sharp knife, carefully trim skin from fish steaks. If steaks are very large, cut them into triangular or square portions, 6 to 8 ounces each. Brush the swordfish on both sides with the remaining oil and grill fish, turning steaks once, until just done, 3 to 4 minutes on each side.

SERVING Transfer fish to serving plates. Divide the tomato mixture over the swordfish and serve immediately.

MAKES ❹ SERVINGS

GRILLED SWORDFISH WITH BEURRE BLANC

To prevent the beurre blanc from melting on the plate, serve it at the side of hot food, rather than on top.

2 tomatoes

Beurre Blanc (recipe follows)

4 swordfish steaks (about 1½ pounds total)

¼ cup chiffonade of basil

Salt and ground black pepper

PREPARATION Peel, seed, and chop the tomatoes. Complete "preparation" in beurre blanc recipe.

COOKING AND SERVING Heat the grill. Cook swordfish on preheated grill until just cooked through and golden on both sides, about 7 minutes total. Meanwhile, cut the basil into thin strips. Finish the beurre blanc. Stir the tomato and basil into the beurre blanc and season to taste. Serve fish with sauce.

MAKES **4** SERVINGS

*B*eurre blanc is a delicate butter sauce that goes especially well with vegetables or poached or steamed fish.

1 shallot

3 tablespoons white-wine vinegar

¼ cup dry white wine

½ pound butter

Salt and ground black pepper

PREPARATION Mince the shallot. Put the vinegar, wine, and shallot in a small, heavy saucepan and boil until liquid has almost evaporated, about 5 minutes. Recipe can be made to this point a few hours ahead.

COOKING Over the lowest possible heat, whisk cold butter into reduction, about a tablespoon at a time, adding another piece as each is almost incorporated. Butter should not melt completely but should soften to form a creamy sauce. If the sauce gets too hot and butter starts to melt, remove it from the heat and continue adding the rest of the cold butter. Season to taste with salt and pepper.

MAKES ❶ CUP

The deep-fried lemon slices in this sandwich are a most successful enhancement to the swordfish.

8 sun-dried plum tomatoes

4 lemons

4 tablespoons flour

4 tablespoons cornmeal

Pinch of salt

1 teaspoon black pepper

1 loaf whole-wheat bread, unsliced

½ cup olive oil

3 cups oil

4 three- to four-ounce swordfish steaks (about ¼ inch thick)

PREPARATION Cut the tomatoes into thin julienne strips. Cut lemons into ⅛- to 1/16-inch thick slices. In a bowl, mix together the flour, cornmeal, and salt and pepper. Recipe can be made to this point several hours ahead.

COOKING AND SERVING Heat the grill or broiler. Cut 8 thick slices of bread and brush each side with 1 tablespoon of olive oil. In a deep fryer or large, heavy saucepan, heat the oil to 375°F. Dredge the lemon slices, a few at a time, in flour mixture and then submerge in hot oil until golden, 45 seconds to 1 minute. Drain. Grill or broil bread on both sides. Arrange fried lemon slices on four slices of bread. Sprinkle with tomatoes. Grill or broil swordfish, turning once, about 2 minutes total for medium-rare on grill, about 3 minutes in broiler. Put a piece of fish on top of each sandwich and cover with a slice of bread. Cut in half and serve warm.

MAKES **4** SERVINGS

TUNA STEAKS WITH CAPER MAYONNAISE

*T**he addition of capers and anchovies to the mayonnaise adds a slightly briny flavor to the fresh tuna.***

Caper Mayonnaise

1 small clove garlic

1 tablespoon capers

2 egg yolks

1 teaspoon Dijon mustard

Salt and coarse pepper

1½ tablespoons lemon juice

½ cup olive oil

5 tablespoons vegetable oil

¼ cup white wine

5 anchovies

4 boneless, ½-inch thick fresh tuna steaks (about 6 ounces each)

Salt and ground black pepper

1 tablespoon capers

PREPARATION *For the mayonnaise*, mince the garlic. Drain, rinse, and chop the capers. Put the egg yolks, mustard, a pinch of salt, ¼ teaspoon pepper, and lemon juice into a food processor or mixing bowl. Process briefly to blend or whisk by hand. With the motor running or while whisking constantly by hand, add the olive oil and ¼ cup of vegetable oil, drop by drop at first and then in a steady stream when the mixture emulsifies. Add capers and process briefly or stir in.

COOKING Heat remaining 1 tablespoon vegetable oil in a skillet until almost smoking. Sprinkle both sides of the tuna with salt and pepper and cook over high heat, turning once, until the tuna is seared well on the outside but still rare on the inside, about 2 minutes total. Remove tuna from the pan and keep warm. Add garlic, wine, and anchovies to the pan and cook over low heat about 30 seconds, mashing anchovies with the back of a spoon. Remove pan from heat. Blend in the mayonnaise.

SERVING Serve tuna topped with mayonnaise. Garnish with capers.

MAKES **4** SERVINGS

GRILLED TUNA WITH BASIL AND RED PEPPERS

~

T he deep red sauce makes a colorful comple-
ment to the tuna. For a fine warm-weather meal, add corn on the cob,
grilled potatoes, and a cool, crisp salad.

2 limes
1²/₃ cups olive oil
4 tuna steaks (about 1¹/₂ pounds
     total)
1 small ripe tomato
3 red bell peppers
1 shallot
15 fresh basil leaves
3 tablespoons red-wine vinegar
Salt
Cayenne pepper

PREPARATION Squeeze juice from limes. In a bowl, whisk together 1 cup of the olive oil and the lime juice. Put the tuna in bowl and marinate at room temperature for about 1 hour. Peel and seed the tomato. Roast red bell peppers over a gas flame, under the broiler, or on the grill until skin blackens and blisters. Cool, remove skin, and seed peppers. Put the shallot, basil, tomato, vinegar, and two of the peppers in the bowl of a food processor and process until smooth. With the machine running, add the remaining ²/₃ cup olive oil in a thin stream. Season to taste with salt and a pinch of cayenne pepper. Chop remaining pepper and add to sauce. (Recipe can be completed to this point several hours ahead.)

COOKING AND SERVING Heat the grill. Remove tuna steaks from marinade and grill, basting with marinade, about 5 minutes for rare. Be sure not to overcook. Top tuna with sauce and serve.

MAKES **4** SERVINGS

MEAT

Beef Tenderloin
with Sage,
Rosemary, and
Arugula
114

Steak with
Mushrooms and
Red-Wine Sauce
115

Grilled Steak
Topped with Pepper
and Garlic Butter
116

Steaks with
Bourbon-Glazed
Onions
117

Veal Chops Sauté
118

Four Onion Relish
119

Veal Scallops in
Lime-Cream Sauce
120

Broiled Lamb Chops
on a Bed of Sautéed
Watercress
121

Grilled Lamb with
Mint Sauce and
Cucumber Raita
122

Pork Cutlets with
Tomato Citrus
Sauce
123

Stir-Fried Pork
with Broccoli
124

Midwest Pork
Tenderloin
Sandwich
125

Sweet Sausage with
Grapes
126

Calf's Liver with
Parsley and Lemon
127

BEEF TENDERLOIN WITH SAGE, ROSEMARY, AND ARUGULA

When tenderloin is sliced into medallions, lightly pounded, and quickly seared, the result is very tender, rare scallops of beef. The beef is sprinkled with minced sage and rosemary and served on a bed of arugula.

1½ pounds center-cut beef
   tenderloin, trimmed
½ tablespoon minced rosemary,
   plus 3 sprigs for garnish
½ tablespoon minced sage, plus 5
   leaves for garnish
2 bunches arugula (about 8 ounces)
7 tablespoons extra-virgin olive oil
1½ tablespoons balsamic vinegar
Salt and ground black pepper

PREPARATION Cut the tenderloin into 12 medallions, each about ³/₄ inch thick. Put each medallion between two pieces of plastic wrap or wax paper and gently pound into ¹/₄-inch thick scallops. Stem and rinse arugula. Arrange arugula on a large serving platter and drizzle with the balsamic vinegar and 5 tablespoons of the oil.

COOKING Brush 2 large skillets with 1 tablespoon of oil. Sear the scallops until rare, about 1 minute on each side.

SERVING Put scallops in a single layer over the arugula and sprinkle with salt, pepper, minced rosemary and sage, and the remaining tablespoon olive oil. Garnish with rosemary sprigs and whole sage leaves.

MAKES **4** SERVINGS

STEAK WITH MUSHROOMS AND RED-WINE SAUCE

teak, mushrooms, and red wine are an unbeatable combination. For a truly elegant dish use wild mushrooms and a specially tender cut of steak.

½ pound mushrooms
3 tablespoons butter
Salt and ground black pepper
2 shallots
¼ cup chopped parsley
1 large *or* 4 individual 1-inch thick
    steak(s) (1½ pounds)
1 cup red wine

PREPARATION Quarter the mushrooms. Melt 2 tablespoons of the butter in a small pan and sauté mushrooms over medium-high heat, stirring, until almost all liquid is evaporated, about 5 minutes. Season to taste with salt and pepper and set aside. Chop the shallots and parsley. (Recipe can be completed to this point several hours ahead.)

COOKING AND SERVING In a large frying pan, melt the remaining tablespoon of butter and sauté the steak(s) over high heat until seared on both sides, about 2 minutes total. Season with salt and pepper. Lower heat to medium and cook, turning once, about 4 more minutes for medium-rare. Put steak(s) on a warm serving platter or individual plates and keep warm. Pour off all but 1 tablespoon of fat from the frying pan. Sauté the shallots in the same pan until soft, about 3 minutes. Add wine, stirring with a wooden spoon to deglaze the pan. Bring to a boil and reduce the liquid to a thick, syrupy sauce, about 3 minutes. Stir in the parsley and sautéed mushrooms. Season to taste with salt and pepper. Top steaks with the sauce and serve immediately.

MAKES **4** SERVINGS

GRILLED STEAK TOPPED WITH PEPPER AND GARLIC BUTTER

G*rilling — every summer's hottest cooking method — makes easy work of these succulent steaks.*

Pepper and Garlic Butter

¹/₄ pound butter

1 red bell pepper

1 tablespoon chopped parsley

2 cloves garlic

Salt and ground black pepper

4³/₄-pound beef steaks

Salt and ground black pepper

PREPARATION Heat grill. *For the butter*, bring butter to room temperature or soften in a microwave. Grill red pepper until skin is charred. Peel and seed. Chop pepper and parsley. Mince garlic. Combine all ingredients.

COOKING Heat grill if not still hot. Season both sides of steaks with salt and pepper. Grill 4 inches from heat source, turning once, about 8 minutes total for medium-rare.

SERVING Put steak on warm plates and top with Pepper and Garlic Butter.

MAKES **4** SERVINGS

STEAKS WITH BOURBON-GLAZED ONIONS

*D**eglazing the pan with bourbon is a fast way to make an elegant dish out of simple pan-fried steaks with onions.*

1 large onion
3 tablespoons butter
½ teaspoon dried thyme
4 ½-pound shell steak *or* rib-eye steaks
Salt and ground black pepper
1 tablespoon oil
3 tablespoons bourbon

PREPARATION Cut the onion into thin slices. Heat 2 tablespoons of the butter in a large, heavy frying pan. Add the onion and cook over very low heat, stirring often, until very soft, about 10 minutes. Add the thyme and raise heat to medium-low. Cook, stirring often, until the onion is golden, about 10 minutes more. Remove the onion with a slotted spoon and set aside.

COOKING Season the steaks with salt and pepper. Add the remaining 1 tablespoon butter and the oil to the pan. Cook the steaks over medium-high heat, turning once, about 6 minutes total for medium-rare. Transfer steaks to warm plates. Add bourbon to pan, stirring with a wooden spoon to deglaze. Return the onion to the pan and toss to coat.

SERVING Put onion and pan juices over the steaks.

MAKES **4** SERVINGS

A sauté's short cooking time means this dish can be prepared entirely at the last minute.

4 large veal chops, trimmed of
    excess fat (about 1½ pounds
    total)
Salt and ground black pepper
4 tablespoons unsalted butter,
    clarified *or* 2 tablespoons
    unsalted butter plus 1 tablespoon
    vegetable oil
2 tablespoons cognac
2 cups red wine
3 tablespoons unsalted butter
Thyme sprigs for garnish
Four-Onion Relish (recipe follows)

PREPARATION Season veal chops with salt and pepper.

COOKING In a heavy frying pan, heat clarified butter or butter and oil until hot. Add veal chops and brown them thoroughly on both sides. Remove pan from heat, add cognac, and flame it carefully. When flame dies down, add wine, cover, and cook on low heat, turning chops halfway through cooking, until veal tests done, about 20 minutes. Remove veal from pan and keep warm. Bring cooking liquid to a boil, skim any fat from surface, strain liquid into a small saucepan, and bring to a simmer. Season to taste with salt and pepper and remove pan from heat. Whisk in 3 tablespoons butter, a little at a time.

SERVING Coat 4 warm plates with sauce and put a veal chop on each plate. Garnish with thyme sprigs and serve with Four-Onion Relish.

MAKES ❹ SERVINGS

FOUR ONION RELISH

꒜

This versatile relish is simplicity itself. The unexpected combination of different onion flavors make this a great complement to veal and other meats.

5 tablespoons unsalted butter

2 leeks, sliced thin

3 scallions, sliced thin

2 large sweet onions, such as Vidalia, sliced thin

1 large red onion, sliced thin

Salt and ground black pepper

½ teaspoon sugar

½ teaspoon minced fresh thyme leaves

COOKING In a large skillet, heat butter. Add leeks, scallions, sweet and red onions, and salt and pepper. Cover and cook, stirring occasionally, over low heat until onions are soft, 15 minutes. Spoon off excess liquid from onions and sprinkle with sugar and thyme. Cook over high heat until onions just begin to brown at edges.

SERVING Serve warm or at room temperature.

MAKES **4** SERVINGS

VEAL SCALLOPS IN LIME-CREAM SAUCE

*T*hin, tender scallops of veal are sauced with a creamy mixture with accents of tangy lime. This dish can be prepared in less than 30 minutes.

Zest of 1 lime, removed in thin
   shreds with a zesting tool
2 tablespoons unsalted butter
1 pound thin veal scallops
Salt and ground black pepper
2 tablespoons white wine
2 tablespoons lime juice
½ cup chicken stock
½ cup heavy cream

COOKING In a saucepan, blanch lime zest 1 minute in boiling water to cover and drain. In a large skillet, heat butter. Season veal lightly with salt and pepper. Sauté veal quickly over medium-high heat about 45 seconds on each side. Do not crowd. Remove from pan. Keep warm. Add wine and lime juice, scraping bottom of pan with a wooden spoon to deglaze. Cook over high heat for about 30 seconds. Add chicken stock and cream, stirring until well combined. Cook over medium-high heat until sauce is thick enough to coat a spoon, about 2 minutes. Season with salt and pepper to taste.

SERVING Spoon some sauce over each serving and sprinkle with lime zest.

MAKES **4** SERVINGS

BROILED LAMB CHOPS ON A BED OF SAUTEED WATERCRESS

The lamb chops are broiled with a light but flavorful rosemary- and parsley-seasoned breading.

1 clove garlic, minced

6 tablespoons unsalted butter

1½ cups fresh bread crumbs

3 tablespoons minced parsley

1 teaspoon minced fresh rosemary leaves *or* ¼ teaspoon dried

Salt and ground black pepper

2 6-rib racks of lamb, cut into 12 chops and trimmed of excess fat (about 2 pounds total)

2 bunches watercress (about ¾ pound), trimmed

2 small scallions, minced

PREPARATION Heat broiler.

COOKING Sauté garlic in 3 tablespoons of the butter in a small skillet over medium heat, for about 1 minute, until soft. Remove from heat. Toss bread crumbs, parsley, rosemary, and salt and pepper with garlic/butter. Sprinkle lamb lightly with salt and pepper. Broil just one side 5 to 6 inches from heat source for 4 minutes. Turn chops and broil 2 minutes. Remove from broiler and top chops with breadcrumb mixture. Return to broiler and broil until mixture is browned and crisp, 2 more minutes. Lamb should be medium-rare. Heat remaining 3 tablespoons butter in a skillet. Add watercress and scallions. Toss over medium-high heat until watercress just begins to wilt, about 1 minute. Season with salt and pepper to taste.

SERVING Divide watercress among 4 serving plates. Arrange lamb chops around watercress. Serve immediately.

MAKES **4** SERVINGS

T

he combination of two sauces — one tangy and fiery, the other cool and creamy — provides an interesting contrast for the grilled lamb cubes.

1 large clove garlic

1¹/₄ pounds boneless leg of lamb cut into 1¹/₄-inch cubes

¹/₄ cup olive oil

1 tablespoon lemon juice

Salt and ground black pepper

Mint Sauce

1 fresh jalapeño

¹/₃ cup fresh cilantro

¹/₂ cup fresh mint leaves

1 teaspoon sugar

Salt

3 tablespoons lemon juice

Cucumber Raita

1 plum tomato

1 small cucumber

¹/₂ cup plain yogurt

¹/₄ teaspoon ground cumin

Salt and ground black pepper

PREPARATION Mince the garlic. Put lamb cubes in a nonreactive container. Add the oil, garlic, lemon juice, ¹/₄ teaspoon salt, and ¹/₈ teaspoon pepper. Turn lamb to coat and marinate at room temperature, turning occasionally, until ready to cook. *For the Mint Sauce*, remove seeds and ribs from the jalapeño. Put the jalapeño, cilantro, mint, sugar, ¹/₄ teaspoon salt, lemon juice, and 2 tablespoons of water in a food processor or blender and puree until smooth. Transfer to a small serving dish and reserve. *For the Cucumber Raita*, halve and seed the tomato. Peel, halve, and seed the cucumber. Chop the tomato and cucumber in a food processor or by hand. Drain. Put tomato and cucumber mixture into a bowl and stir in the yogurt and cumin. Season to taste with salt and pepper. Recipe can be done to this point several hours ahead.

COOKING AND SERVING Heat the grill. Thread the lamb cubes on skewers and grill until browned but still pink inside, about 8 minutes. Put skewered lamb on plates and serve sauces on the side.

MAKES **4** SERVINGS

PORK CUTLETS WITH TOMATO CITRUS SAUCE

꿍

he fresh, crisp flavor of tomato and orange combine perfectly in the unusual sauce that accompanies these breaded slices of tender pork.

4 slices rye bread
1 pound boneless loin of pork
1/4 cup flour
Salt and ground black pepper
1 egg
1 shallot
1 orange
5 plum tomatoes
4 tablespoons butter
1 tablespoon oil
1/4 cup white wine

PREPARATION In a food processor, process the bread slices to make about 1 1/2 cups of fine crumbs. Cut the pork into 1/4-inch thick slices. In a shallow dish, combine the flour, 1/2 teaspoon salt, and 1/4 teaspoon pepper. In another shallow dish, lightly beat the egg. Put breadcrumbs into a third shallow dish. Dip the pork pieces into the flour mixture. Shake off excess flour, dip into the egg, and then into the bread crumbs to coat completely. Mince the shallot. Grate 1 1/2 teaspoons zest from the orange. Squeeze 1/4 cup orange juice. Seed and chop the tomatoes. Recipe can be done to this point 1 hour ahead.

COOKING AND SERVING In a large skillet, heat 2 tablespoons of the butter and the oil. Sauté the breaded pork on both sides over medium heat until golden brown and cooked through, about 5 minutes total. Remove pork from pan and keep warm. Melt the remaining 2 tablespoons of butter in the pan and sauté the shallot for 30 seconds. Add the orange juice and wine, stirring with a wooden spoon to deglaze the bottom on the pan. Cook over medium heat until reduced by half, about 2 minutes. Add the tomatoes and simmer gently over low heat until lightly thickened, about 5 minutes. Stir in orange zest and season to taste with salt and pepper. Put the sauce on plates and top with pork.

MAKES **4** SERVINGS

*R*ub the pork lightly with cornstarch to seal
the meat before frying. This recipe can be used as a guide for other
stir-fries, in which poultry, shellfish, or quick cooking vegetables such as
snow peas, cabbage, mushrooms, or green beans are substituted for the
pork. Cashews and other nuts are a welcome addition to any stir-fry.

Sauce

4 teaspoons dark soy sauce

2 teaspoons sugar

2 teaspoons cornstarch

2 teaspoons Chinese red- or white-
wine vinegar

2 teaspoons rice wine *or* dry sherry

2 teaspoons Oriental sesame oil

Pork and Vegetables

2½ teaspoons cornstarch

2 tablespoons chicken stock *or*
water

1 pound boneless pork loin *or*
tenderloin

1 bunch broccoli (about 12 ounces)

1 large red bell pepper

4 scallions

1 medium garlic clove

1 piece ginger, about 1 inch long

4 tablespoons vegetable oil

½ cup cashews (2 ounces)

PREPARATION *For the sauce*, mix the soy sauce, sugar, cornstarch, vinegar, rice wine, sesame oil, and ¼ teaspoon salt
in a small bowl. Set aside. *For the pork and vegetables*,
dissolve 1½ teaspoons of cornstarch in the chicken stock.
Set aside. Slice the pork thinly against the grain and rub with
remaining teaspoon of cornstarch. Cut broccoli into small
florets and blanch in a large kettle of boiling water until
almost tender, about 3 minutes. Drain well and pat dry. Cut
the red pepper into ¼-inch strips and set aside. Thinly slice
the scallions, mince the garlic (1 teaspoon), and the ginger
(1½ tablespoons); set each aside.

COOKING In a wok or deep skillet, heat 2 tablespoons oil until
hot but not smoking. Stir-fry the red peppers and cashews
until peppers soften slightly and cashews start to brown,
about 30 seconds; remove and set aside. Add pork and
stir-fry until seared on both sides, about 1 minute; remove
and set aside with the peppers. Heat the remaining 2 tablespoons of oil, add the garlic, scallions, and ginger, and
stir-fry until fragrant, about 15 seconds. Return the red
peppers, cashews, and pork to the wok. Immediately stir in
broccoli, sauce, and cornstarch-chicken stock mixture.
Toss until sauce coats ingredients and thickens slightly,
about 45 seconds. Serve immediately with steamed rice.

MAKES **4** SERVINGS

MIDWEST PORK TENDERLOIN SANDWICH

The tenderloin sandwich — the definitive Midwestern sandwich — is a celebration of pork. Its preparation is not fancy, but it is doted on by legions of fans, who debate which cafe makes the widest, the thinnest, the crispest.

1 pound boneless, center-cut loin of pork

1 cup flour

Salt and ground black pepper

Oil for frying

1/2 cup yellow cornmeal, approximately

4 hamburger buns

Condiments, such as mustard and mayonnaise (optional)

PREPARATION Cut four 1-inch slices of pork. Trim fat from the edges and butterfly each slice by cutting horizontally through the middle almost to the edge so that the halves are connected by only a thin piece of meat. Put each butterflied slice between pieces of lightly oiled parchment or plastic wrap. Using a wooden mallet or the side of a cleaver, pound vigorously until the slice is about 10 inches across. Mix flour with about 1 teaspoon salt and 1/2 teaspoon pepper.

COOKING Heat 1/2 inch of oil in a deep frying pan to 375°F. Dip each slice of pork in water, then in flour mixture. Pat both sides with cornmeal. Fry tenderloin, turning once, until golden brown on both sides, about 5 minutes total. Drain the pork on paper towels and season to taste with salt and pepper.

SERVING Serve on buns with optional condiments.

MAKES 4 SERVINGS

The light, fresh flavor of the grapes provides a subtle contrast with the robust sausages in this unusual combination. It goes well with hot, buttered noodles.

2 pounds red *or* green seedless
   grapes
2 pounds sweet Italian sausages *or*
   other link sausage

PREPARATION Halve grapes. Cut sausages on an angle into 1 inch-long pieces. Recipe can be made to this point several hours ahead.

COOKING AND SERVING Heat a large frying pan over medium heat and cook the sausages until brown but not cooked through, about 5 minutes. Lower heat to medium-low, stir in grapes, cover, and continue cooking, stirring occasionally, until sausages are cooked through and grapes have released their juice, about 20 minutes. Uncover pan, raise heat to high, and cook until juices have thickened a bit, about 5 minutes. Serve immediately.

MAKES 4 SERVINGS

CALF'S LIVER WITH PARSLEY AND LEMON

Sliced calf's or veal liver is one of the quickest cooking cuts, but one that produces very satisfying results.

1 pound calf's *or* veal liver
1 cup flour
¼ cup chopped parsley
4 tablespoons butter
1 lemon

PREPARATION Cut liver on an angle into slices about ¼ inch thick and coat lightly with flour. Chop parsley.

COOKING Melt 2 tablespoons of the butter in a skillet over medium heat, add the liver slices, and brown on both sides, about 1 minute total. Transfer to warm plates. Pour off excess butter. Melt remaining 2 tablespoons butter in the same skillet. Squeeze in juice from lemon and remove pan from heat. Add the parsley and shake pan to combine. Pour butter over liver.

MAKES **4** SERVINGS

Poultry

Perfect Fried
Chicken
130

Rosemary Fried
Chicken
131

Chili-Spiced Fried
Chicken
132

Fried Chicken Salad
with Sweet Onions
133

Grilled Chicken on
Arugula Salad
134

Chicken Salad with
Thyme and Red
Onion Vinaigrette
135

Chicken with
Smoked Mozzarella
and Pesto
136

Grilled Chicken
Breasts with
Cilantro-Lime
Butter
137

Chicken with
Mushrooms and
Garlic
138

Sautéed Chicken
with Tarragon and
Mushrooms
139

Chicken Breasts
with Summer
Squash and Yellow
Peppers
140

Steamed Breast of
Chicken with Red-
Onion Marmalade
141

Chicken Stuffed
with Blue Cheese
and Walnuts
142

Broiled Ginger-
Orange Game Hens
143

Grilled Ginger Duck
Breasts with
Peaches
144

PERFECT FRIED CHICKEN
❧

frying chicken should weigh about 2¹/₂ pounds minus giblets. It should be disjointed, not hack-sawed into quarters. The bony back pieces will become hotly contested for, once they're fried to crispy deliciousness.

2 frying chickens (each about 2¹/₂ pounds)
1 quart milk, approximately
1 teaspoon hot red-pepper sauce
2 cups flour, approximately
2 tablespoons coarse salt
Ground black pepper
Vegetable oil for frying

PREPARATION Disjoint chickens so that you have 4 thighs, 4 drumsticks, 4 breast halves, 4 wings, and 2 pieces of bony back. Cut chicken backbones in half crosswise. Bash the breast pieces with the flat part of a cleaver to flatten them for quicker and more even cooking. Cut each half-breast once again across horizontally. Soak chicken in milk seasoned with hot red-pepper sauce for 15 to 20 minutes. Put flour into a paper bag, add salt and pepper, and shake well.

COOKING Heat ¹/₂-inch oil in 1 or 2 large, heavy, iron frying pan(s) over high heat until hot but not smoking. Shake thighs and drumsticks in bag, shake off each piece, pat so that flour adheres, and slide into hot oil. (A splatter screen is immensely helpful.) Fry thighs and drumsticks about 20 minutes total as follows: fry about 3 minutes and reduce heat to medium-low. Fry on medium-low for 5 to 7 minutes and then turn chicken with tongs. Turn heat up for a few minutes, and then turn it down to medium-low. Continue frying on medium low for 10 more minutes, turning once. Drain on crumpled paper towels. Continue frying remaining chicken in same manner, except that small breast halves or quarters should be fried for no more than a total of 15 minutes. Wings and back pieces need 20 minutes.

SERVING Serve as soon as possible. You can keep the dark meat, which is fried first, warm in a low oven very briefly, but it will become soggy if left too long.

MAKES **4** SERVINGS

T*he fried rosemary sprigs will flavor the chicken to a surprising degree, and they are good to eat, too.*

1 4-pound chicken
1 cup flour
Salt and coarse black pepper
Oil for frying
Fresh rosemary sprigs

PREPARATION Cut the chicken into 8 pieces. Combine the flour with 1 tablespoon salt and 2 teaspoons pepper. Dip the chicken pieces in water and dredge in flour mixture.

COOKING AND SERVING In a frying pan, heat about $1\frac{1}{2}$ inches of oil over high heat to 375°F. Add the chicken. When the temperature returns to 375°F, lower heat to medium. Cook until golden brown on both sides and almost done, about 15 minutes. Raise heat to medium-high and finish browning, about 5 minutes more. During the last couple of minutes of frying, add a few fresh rosemary sprigs and fry until just crisp, about 2 minutes. Drain chicken and rosemary sprigs and serve at once.

MAKES 4 SERVINGS

*R*ubbing the spice mixture onto the chicken skin and refrigerating the chicken overnight before cooking will intensify the flavor. The spices may be omitted to make plain fried chicken or mixtures such as curry powder and cumin or mixed provençal herbs can be substituted for the spice blend in the recipe.

8 chicken drumsticks (3 pounds)
8 wings (2 pounds)
3 tablespoons chili powder
2 tablespoons ground cumin
2 teaspoons turmeric
1 teaspoon cayenne pepper
Salt and ground black pepper
6 eggs
1/2 teaspoon hot red-pepper sauce
2 1/2 cups plain dry breadcrumbs
1 1/3 cups all-purpose flour
3 cups vegetable oil
2 lemons

PREPARATION Rinse and pat chicken pieces dry. Cut off wing tips (can reserve for stock). Grasp each side of the remaining wing sections and fold them backwards to crack the joint and permit them to lie flat in the skillet. Mix the spices with 1/2 teaspoon salt and 1/2 teaspoon ground black pepper, then rub the mixture over chicken pieces. Beat eggs with hot-pepper sauce in a shallow bowl. Put breadcrumbs on a large plate. Dredge chicken pieces in flour. Dip pieces in the eggs, then roll in breadcrumbs.

COOKING AND SERVING Heat 1 1/2 cups oil in each of two 10-inch skillets to 275°F. Add chicken to skillets without crowding. Slowly brown chicken over medium-low heat, turning as needed, until juices run clear, about 12 minutes for wings and about 20 minutes for legs. Transfer fried chicken to a paper towel-lined baking sheet and keep warm in a 250°F oven. Remove any browned bits of coating from skillets to prevent burning, add oil as needed, and repeat to fry remaining chicken pieces. Cut lemons into wedges and serve with chicken.

MAKES 4 SERVINGS

Fried Chicken Salad with Sweet Onions

~

Traditional fried chicken, served on a bed of lettuce leaves and cherry tomatoes and garnished with capers and tarragon leaves, is a perfect example of the new southern cuisine.

2 heads Boston *or* Bibb lettuce

8 cherry tomatoes, halved

1/2 cup peanut oil

1/2 cup all-purpose flour

Salt and ground black pepper

1/4 teaspoon coarse-ground black pepper

1/3 cup milk

2 whole broiler-fryer chicken breasts, halved, boned, and cut into 1/2-inch wide strips

2 tablespoons white wine vinegar

2 teaspoons Dijon mustard

1/2 cup sliced mushrooms

1 shallot, minced

1 tablespoon chopped tarragon leaves *or* 1 teaspoon dried

1 tablespoon capers, drained (optional)

1 sweet onion, such as Vidalia, sliced thin

Tarragon leaves for garnish

PREPARATION Arrange lettuce leaves and tomatoes on 4 salad plates. Heat oil in a skillet on medium-high heat. In a shallow bowl, mix flour with 1/2 teaspoon salt and coarse pepper. Put milk in another bowl. Dip chicken strips into milk and then into flour mixture to coat.

COOKING Fry chicken on both sides until golden brown, about 5 minutes total. Drain chicken on paper towels, reserving oil in the pan. Add vinegar to oil. Stir, scraping pan to deglaze. Pour oil and vinegar into a mixing bowl, add mustard, and mix. Add mushrooms, shallot, and tarragon and season to taste.

SERVING To serve, put chicken strips on lettuce leaves and pour on just enough vinaigrette to moisten leaves. Scatter capers and sliced onion on top of salads. Garnish with tarragon leaves. Serve remaining dressing on the side.

MAKES 4 SERVINGS

GRILLED CHICKEN ON
ARUGULA SALAD

The hot, grilled chicken is served on a bed of arugula which has been tossed in a warm pimiento dressing.

Pimiento Dressing
¼ cup minced pimiento
¼ cup olive oil
2 tablespoons balsamic *or* other
   mild vinegar
Salt and coarse-ground black
   pepper

2 bunches arugula (about 1 pound)
¼ cup olive oil
Salt and coarse black pepper
8 boneless, skinless chicken thighs
   (about 1⅓ pounds)

PREPARATION *For the dressing*, mince the pimiento. Combine the pimiento with the olive oil and vinegar in a nonreactive pan and season to taste with salt and pepper. Stem, wash, and gently dry the arugula. Combine the olive oil, 1 teaspoon salt, and ½ teaspoon pepper in a large bowl. Coat the chicken with the oil mixture, reserving some for later use.

COOKING AND SERVING Heat the grill or broiler. On the grill, sear both sides of the chicken and then move to a cooler part of the grill. Cook, turning once, until just cooked through, about 25 minutes total. Broil about 15 minutes. Baste frequently with remaining oil/salt mixture. Near the end of cooking, put the dressing on the side of the grill or over very low heat to warm. Cut the chicken into thick slices. Toss the arugula with the warm dressing and top with chicken slices.

MAKES 4 SERVINGS

P

CHICKEN SALAD WITH THYME AND RED ONION VINAIGRETTE

ungent thyme is a natural accompaniment to sweet red onion in this salad. You can serve the salad warm or prepare it a few hours ahead of time and serve it at room temperature.

1 small red onion
½ head romaine lettuce
½ head red-leaf lettuce
4 large or 6 medium boneless, skinless chicken breasts (about 1½ pounds)
1 tablespoon minced fresh thyme
Salt and ground black pepper
⅓ cup oil
3 tablespoons balsamic *or* red wine vinegar

PREPARATION Cut onion into paper-thin slices and separate into rings. Wash and spin-dry lettuces; tear leaves into pieces and chill. Cut chicken into 1-inch cubes and sprinkle with thyme and salt and pepper. Heat ½ of the oil in a large skillet over medium-high heat until hot but not smoking. Add the chicken and sauté, stirring frequently, until just cooked through, about 5 minutes. Remove chicken and set aside. Add the vinegar to skillet, stirring with a wooden spoon to deglaze the bottom of the pan. Remove skillet from heat and stir in the onion and remaining oil. Season to taste with salt and pepper. (Recipe can be prepared to this point a few hours ahead.) Set chicken and vinaigrette aside separately in covered containers.

SERVING Arrange chilled lettuce on salad plates and top with chicken and red onion vinaigrette.

MAKES 4 SERVINGS

P

CHICKEN WITH SMOKED
MOZZARELLA AND PESTO

esto and smoked mozzarella make a delicious stuffing for chicken breasts in this satisfying dish.

Pesto
1/2 cup fresh basil leaves
1 tablespoon pine nuts
1 tablespoon grated Parmesan
1/2 clove garlic
1/4 cup olive oil, approximately

4 boneless, skinless chicken
   breasts
4 1/4-inch slices smoked mozzarella
   (about 3 ounces)
2 tablespoons oil
1 tablespoon butter
Flour for dressing

PREPARATION *For the pesto*, combine the basil, pine nuts, Parmesan cheese, and garlic in a food processor and pulse until minced. With the machine running, slowly add olive oil, up to 1/4 cup, to form a paste. (Pesto can be made several days ahead.) Make a pocket in each chicken breast by cutting horizontally into the side. Make each incision about 3/4 the length of the breast. Fill pockets with the pesto and mozzarella and trim any cheese that is not totally enclosed. (Recipe can be made to this point 1 day ahead.)

COOKING AND SERVING Heat oil and butter in a skillet over medium-high heat. Dredge the chicken in flour and shake off excess. Sauté chicken in butter and oil for about 5 minutes. Turn the chicken, lower heat to medium-low, and continue cooking until cooked through, about 4 minutes. Serve immediately.

MAKES **4** SERVINGS

T

GRILLED CHICKEN BREASTS
WITH CILANTRO-LIME BUTTER

✗

he first joint of the wing is like a jaunty little drumstick that makes grilled or broiled chicken breasts seem particularly substantial and attractive. Approximately half the herb butter is used in the recipe; the remainder can be reserved or frozen for use on fish, vegetables such as green beans or broccoli, or in soup. Chicken breasts also may be marinated in garlic, olive oil, and mint, and served with mint butter.

Cilantro-Lime Butter

6 tablespoons softened butter

1 small lime

1 small shallot

3 tablespoons minced cilantro
     leaves

Salt and ground black pepper

1/8 teaspoon cayenne pepper

Chicken and Marinade

2 whole, split chicken breasts with
     wings, skin, and bones (about

1 1/2 pounds)

Salt and ground black pepper

1 medium lime

2 tablespoons olive oil

1 1/2 tablespoons cilantro leaves

PREPARATION *For the cilantro-lime butter,* cream the butter. Grate 1/2 teaspoon zest and squeeze 1 1/2 teaspoons juice from the lime. Beat zest and juice into butter. Peel, mince, and stir in shallot. Stir in cilantro, 1/4 teaspoon salt, 1/4 teaspoon black pepper, and cayenne pepper. Transfer mixture to a sheet of plastic wrap and roll into a 1-inch log; set aside. (Can refrigerate overnight or freeze up to 1 month). *For chicken and marinade,* remove top two-thirds of each wing (can reserve for stock), leaving segment nearest the breast attached. Cut off the knobby wing joints and scrape around the bones. Sprinkle with 1 teaspoon salt and 1/4 teaspoon pepper. Squeeze 2 tablespoons lime juice into a nonreactive baking dish. Stir in oil and cilantro; coat each side of breasts in marinade. Set chicken aside at room temperature for 2 hours. (Can cover and refrigerate overnight.)

COOKING AND SERVING Heat a grill, or adjust oven rack to high position and heat broiler. Grill or broil chicken breasts until juices run clear when pierced in thickest part of breast, turning once, 7 to 8 minutes per side. Transfer chicken to dinner plates and top each with a tablespoon of herb butter.

MAKES ● SERVINGS

ither white or brown rice is a perfect accom-paniment for this tasty dish which cooks quickly in the microwave.

4 skinless, boneless chicken
    breasts

1 can straw mushrooms (1½
    ounces)

2 ounces fresh mushrooms

4 scallions

4 cloves garlic

4 slices of fresh ginger

½ ounce dried tree-ear mushrooms

1 ounce dried shiitake mushrooms

¼ teaspoon dried red-pepper
    flakes

¼ cup tamari *or* other soy sauce

3 tablespoons mirin (sweet rice
    wine)

1 teaspoon toasted sesame oil

1½ cups chicken stock

3 tablespoons cornstarch

PREPARATION Cut chicken into 2-inch chunks. Drain and rinse the straw mushrooms. Remove stems from fresh mushrooms and cut caps into ½-inch-thick slices. Reserve stems for another use. Trim scallions and cut into 2-inch lengths, including green part. Slice the garlic. Peel the ginger and cut into 4 thin slices and then into julienne. In a 2-quart microwaveable container, cook 2 cups of water in the microwave on high for 2 minutes. Remove from microwave and add the tree-ear mushrooms. Stir to moisten and let stand for at least 5 minutes. Drain mushrooms and put into an 2½-quart microwaveable baking dish. Remove stems from the shiitake mushrooms and break caps into quarters and stir into tree-ear mushrooms. Stir in the straw and fresh mushrooms, scallions, garlic, ginger, dried red-pepper flakes, tamari, mirin, sesame oil, and chicken stock. Stir chicken into mushroom mixture and cover with plastic wrap. (Recipe can be completed to this point a few hours ahead.)

COOKING AND SERVING Cook on high for 5 minutes. Meanwhile, dissolve the cornstarch in ¼ cup of cold water. Without removing dish from oven, pierce plastic with the tip of a small knife and stir in dissolved cornstarch with a wooden spoon. Patch plastic and cook on high until sauce is thick, about 5 more minutes. Remove from oven and serve.

MAKES **4** SERVINGS

SAUTÉED CHICKEN WITH TARRAGON AND MUSHROOMS

arragon adds a traditional finish to this delicate white wine and cream sauced sauté.

¼ pound mushrooms (about ¾ cup)

8 chicken thighs (about 2 pounds)

Salt and ground black pepper

2 tablespoons butter

⅓ cup white wine

1 cup heavy cream

1 tablespoon minced fresh tarragon

PREPARATION Rinse, trim, and slice the mushrooms. Sprinkle the chicken lightly with salt and pepper. Melt the butter in a large, nonreactive skillet and cook chicken over medium-high heat until seared on all sides, about 4 minutes. Add mushrooms and cook until softened, about 4 minutes. Stir in wine and reduce heat. Cover and simmer until chicken is cooked through, about 20 minutes. Using a slotted spoon, remove chicken from the pan. Increase heat to high, stir in the cream, and simmer until liquid reduces to ¾ cup, about 4 minutes. Lower heat to medium, return chicken to pan, and continue cooking until chicken is warmed through. Stir in fresh tarragon and season to taste with salt and pepper. Recipe can be prepared several hours ahead.

SERVING Reheat over low heat if made ahead. Serve with rice pilaf, if desired.

MAKES 4 SERVINGS

CHICKEN BREASTS WITH SUMMER SQUASH AND YELLOW PEPPER

The white Lillet aperitif adds a spirited touch to this seasonal sauté. The squash and yellow pepper provide a summery flavor.

1½ pounds skinned, boned chicken breasts

Salt and ground black pepper

2 summer squash

4 tablespoons unsalted butter, clarified *or* 2 tablespoons unsalted butter plus 1 tablespoon vegetable oil

¾ cup white Lillet aperitif

Thin zest of 1 orange, cut off in 1 long strip

1 cup heavy cream

1 yellow bell pepper, cored, seeded, and then cut into ¼- by 1½-inch strips

1½ tablespoons minced fresh mint leaves

Mint sprigs for garnish (optional)

PREPARATION Remove tendon from each chicken breast and pound breasts to flatten them. Season with salt and pepper. Cut peeling from the squash in strips and then cut strips crosswise into thin shreds. Reserve squash for another use.

COOKING In a heavy skillet, heat clarified butter or butter and oil over medium-high heat. Sear chicken on both sides, about 2 minutes in all. Add Lillet and orange zest and cook until sauce is reduced to about 2 tablespoons. Discard zest and add cream. Turn breasts over and stir in squash peel and bell pepper. Cook, turning breasts often, until chicken just tests done and vegetables are tender, about 3 minutes.

SERVING Coat 4 warm plates with sauce, including vegetables. Cut chicken breasts diagonally into thick slices, arrange on plates, and sprinkle with chopped mint. Garnish with mint sprigs. Serve.

MAKES **4** SERVINGS

Steamed Breast of Chicken with Red-Onion Marmalade

✗

Pungent thyme is a natural accompaniment to sweet red onion in this salad. You can serve the salad warm, or prepare it a few hours ahead and serve it at room temperature.

Red-Onion Marmalade
2 red onions, sliced

1 teaspoon olive oil

2 teaspoons sugar

2 teaspoons sherry vinegar

2 cups unsalted, fat-free chicken broth

5 sprigs tarragon

1½ pounds skinless, boneless chicken breasts

2 oranges, peeled and sliced thin

COOKING *For the marmalade,* cook onions, olive oil, and sugar in a skillet over low heat for 20 to 25 minutes. Add vinegar and cook, stirring, until onions are caramelized, about 10 minutes. Bring chicken stock and 1 sprig tarragon to a boil in a saucepan with a rack for steaming. Put chicken on the rack, cover, and steam until chicken just tests done, 5 to 7 minutes. Remove chicken and keep warm. Reduce stock over high heat, uncovered, until it is slightly syrupy, about 15 minutes. Strain and keep warm.

SERVING Slice chicken breasts diagonally against the grain. Arrange orange slices on 4 plates. Fan chicken slices out on bed of orange slices. Top with reduced stock. Spoon the onion marmalade beside the chicken and garnish with the remaining tarragon.

MAKES 4 SERVINGS

CHICKEN STUFFED WITH BLUE CHEESE AND WALNUTS

*M*oist chicken thighs are filled with a flavorful cheese and nut stuffing. Pecans may be used instead of walnuts.

2 ounces walnuts (½ cup chopped)

2 ounces blue cheese (about ½ cup)

1 tablespoon heavy cream

8 large boneless chicken thighs (about 1½ pounds)

Salt and ground black pepper

1 tablespoon butter, softened

PREPARATION Chop the walnuts. Mash the blue cheese with a fork and add about 1 tablespoon of the cream. Mix in half of the walnuts. Shape into eight fairly flat ovals, cover, and chill in the freezer if you're in a hurry. The stuffing can be made and shaped several days ahead. Put the chicken thighs skin side down on a work surface. Pound the flesh lightly to flatten. Season with salt and pepper. Put a chilled cheese oval in the middle of each thigh, wrap the chicken around it, and secure the stuffed chicken with a toothpick, small skewer, or piece of string. Put in an ovenproof pan and dot with butter. (Recipe can be completed to this point several hours ahead.)

COOKING AND SERVING Heat oven to 400°F. Bake chicken in preheated oven, basting once or twice with pan juices, until golden brown, about 30 minutes. Put chicken on plates. Stir remaining walnuts into pan juices and spoon over chicken.

MAKES **4** SERVINGS

BROILED GINGER-ORANGE GAME HENS

~

*T*his delicious and elegant main dish is made in less than thirty minutes. Game hens may also be grilled.

6 tablespoons butter, softened

3 tablespoons grated orange zest

2 tablespoons minced fresh ginger

Salt and ground black pepper

2 Cornish game hens, split (about 2½ pounds)

8 ounces cranberries

⅓ cup sugar

½ cup orange juice

3 tablespoons white wine

PREPARATION Heat broiler. In a bowl, combine butter, 2 tablespoons of the orange zest, and 1 tablespoon of the ginger. Lightly salt and pepper hens inside and out. Using your fingers, loosen skin of hens from flesh. Put 1 tablespoon of the flavored butter underneath skin of each hen. Dot hens with about ½ of the remaining butter.

COOKING Broil about 6 inches from heat source, skin side up, for 10 to 12 minutes. Turn, brush with remaining butter, and broil until just done, 10 to 12 more minutes. Remove from pan and keep warm. Reserve drippings. While hens are broiling, combine cranberries, sugar, orange juice, remaining 1 tablespoon orange zest, and remaining 1 tablespoon ginger in a saucepan. Bring to a boil, stirring to dissolve sugar. Lower heat and simmer until cranberries have all popped and mixture is lightly thickened, about 10 minutes. Set aside. Put pan with drippings over high heat and add wine, stirring until bubbly and slightly syrupy, about 1 minute.

SERVING Spoon pan juices over hens and serve with a spoonful of cranberries.

MAKES 4 SERVINGS

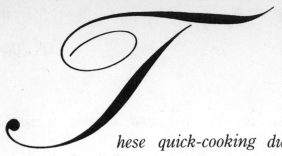

GRILLED GINGER DUCK BREASTS WITH PEACHES

*T*hese quick-cooking duck breasts with their peach garnish, would go well with a pecan-studded rice pilaf.

2 tablespoons dry sherry

2 tablespoons soy sauce

2 tablespoons peanut oil

1 tablespoon minced fresh ginger

Salt and ground black pepper

2 whole duck breasts, boned, skinned, and split (about 1 pound total)

2 ripe, firm peaches

PREPARATION In a shallow, nonreactive dish, combine sherry, soy sauce, oil, and ginger. Lightly salt and pepper duck breasts and put into marinade. Set aside about 15 minutes, turning occasionally. While duck is marinating, heat grill. Halve and pit peaches. Brush peach halves with some of the marinade and place cut side down at outer edge of preheated grill.

COOKING Grill peaches for 2 minutes, brush with marinade, turn, and grill until peaches just begin to soften, about 2 more minutes. While grilling peaches, drain duck and put on hotter part of grill. Grill until medium rare, 2 to 2$^{1}/_{2}$ minutes per side, brushing with remaining marinade before turning.

SERVING Transfer duck and peaches to a warm platter or individual plates.

MAKES **4** SERVINGS

VEGETABLES

Mashed Potatoes
with Roasted Shallot
Hollandaise
148

Hollandaise Sauce
149

Leeks with Vinegar
Sauce
150

Eggplant, Zucchini,
and Bell Pepper
Sauté
151

Sugar-Snap Peas
with Scallions
152

Simple Green Beans
153

Lemon Carrots
154

Kale Timbales with
Sautéed Radishes
155

Sautéed Radishes
156

Country-Style Lima
Beans
157

Sauté of Tomatoes
158

Sautéed
Mushrooms with
Garlic
159

Parsnips with
Orange Juice and
Ham
160

Parsley Fritters
161

Asparagus with
Country Ham and
Lemon Butter
162

Asparagus Bundles
with Cornichon
Vinaigrette
163

Sautéed Broccoli
Rabe with Garlic
164

Spicy Stir-Fried
Eggplant
165

Carrots, Peppers,
and Cabbage in
Lettuce Cups
166

Browned Brussels
Sprouts
167

Sautéed Zucchini
with Walnuts
168

Vegetable Medley
with Green-Pea and
Mint Sauce
169

Green-Pea and Mint
Sauce
170

Vegetables with
Eggs
171

MASHED POTATOES WITH ROASTED SHALLOT HOLLANDAISE

Topping mashed potatoes with hollandaise may sound like gilding the lily, but wait until you try it — decadence never tasted better. Baking potatoes give good results in this dish.

4 shallots

1 tablespoon olive oil

Salt and ground black pepper

4 large potatoes (about 2 pounds)

Hollandaise Sauce (recipe follows)

⅓ cup heavy cream

3 tablespoons butter

⅓ cup milk

PREPARATION Heat oven to 500°F. Toss unpeeled shallots with olive oil and 1 tablespoon salt and roast in preheated oven until soft, stirring occasionally, about 25 minutes. Cool, skin, and mince. Recipe can be made to this point several hours ahead.

COOKING AND SERVING Peel potatoes and cut into quarters. Put potatoes in a pot with cold, salted water to cover, bring to a boil, and cook until tender, about 20 minutes. Drain. Meanwhile, make Hollandaise Sauce and add the minced roasted shallots. Put potatoes through a ricer or mash. In a saucepan, combine the potatoes with the heavy cream, butter, milk, and salt and pepper to taste and heat over medium-low heat, stirring constantly. Serve potatoes topped with hollandaise.

MAKES 4 SERVINGS

HOLLANDAISE SAUCE

verheating hollandaise can cook the egg yolks and make the sauce separate. Hollandaise is best if made just before serving, but it can be made ahead if it is kept in a warm water bath and whisked periodically.

6 ounces butter

3 egg yolks

2 tablespoons water

Salt and ground black pepper

2 teaspoons lemon juice,
    approximately

COOKING Melt the butter. In a small, heavy saucepan over the lowest possible heat, whisk the egg yolks with the water, $1/2$ teaspoon salt, and $1/4$ teaspoon pepper. Whisk constantly until the mixture is light and creamy. Remove from heat and gradually whisk in the warm butter in a thin stream. Stir in lemon juice to taste and salt and pepper if needed. To keep the sauce for a short time, set the pan in a larger pan half filled with warm water.

MAKES ❶ CUP

LEEKS WITH VINEGAR SAUCE

A good side dish, such as this one, can be *just the thing you need to round out a simple meal.*

8 slender leeks

1⅓ cups chicken stock, approximately

Salt and ground black pepper

2 tablespoons balsamic *or* other mild vinegar

4 tablespoons butter

PREPARATION Wash and trim the leeks. Slice leeks, including 1 inch of the green part, on an angle into approximately $1^{1}/_{2}$-inch pieces.

COOKING AND SERVING Put leeks in a skillet just large enough to hold them in a single layer. Add stock to come halfway up the leeks. Add $^{1}/_{8}$ teaspoon pepper. Bring to a simmer, partially cover, and cook over low heat, turning occasionally, until leeks are tender, about 15 minutes. Remove leeks from the pan and keep warm. Remove all but 2 tablespoons cooking liquid. Add the vinegar to the pan and cook until mixture is reduced by $^{1}/_{2}$, about 1 minute. Over lowest heat possible, whisk in the butter bit by bit until it softens to form a creamy sauce but does not melt completely. Season to taste with salt and pepper. Serve the leeks coated with the sauce.

MAKES **4** SERVINGS

EGGPLANT, ZUCCHINI, AND BELL-PEPPER SAUTE

colorful combination of eggplant, zuc-chini, red bell peppers, and basil, all at their peak of flavor, makes this a popular side dish.

1 small red bell pepper
1 small eggplant
1 small zucchini
3¹/₂ tablespoons olive oil
2 tablespoons chopped basil *or* parsley
1 tablespoon butter
Salt and ground black pepper

PREPARATION Cut the red bell pepper, eggplant, and zucchini into approximately 2¹/₂- by ¹/₃-inch strips. In a skillet, heat 1¹/₂ tablespoons of the olive oil over medium-high heat until hot but not smoking. Sauté the eggplant until lightly browned and soft, about 3 minutes. Remove the eggplant from the skillet and set aside. Heat another tablespoon of olive oil in the same pan and sauté the red bell pepper for about 1 minute. Add the remaining tablespoon oil and the zucchini strips and sauté for about 1 minute. Return the eggplant to the pan. Recipe can be made to this point a day ahead.

COOKING AND SERVING Chop the basil. Reheat the sautéed vegetables if made ahead. Stir in the butter and basil, season to taste with salt and black pepper, and cook 1 more minute.

MAKES 4 SERVINGS

T he garden-fresh sugar-snap peas are given a very subtle Oriental flavoring in this simple preparation which takes less than 15 minutes, from start to finish.

2 scallions
½ pound sugar-snap peas
1 tablespoon peanut oil
1 tablespoon soy sauce
A few drops sesame oil

PREPARATION Chop the scallions. String the peas. Blanch peas in boiling, salted water until tender, about 5 minutes. Drain. **COOKING AND SERVING** Heat the peanut oil in a frying pan or wok, add the peas, and stir-fry over medium-high heat for 3 minutes. Stir in the soy sauce, sesame oil, and chopped scallions. Serve warm.

MAKES 4 SERVINGS

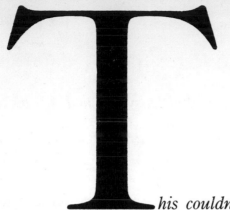

his couldn't-be-quicker side dish lets the flavor of fresh green beans shine through.

2 pounds green beans
4 tablespoons butter
Salt and ground black pepper

PREPARATION Trim the beans and cook in a large pot of boiling, salted water until tender, about 6 minutes. Drain, refresh under cold, running water, and drain well. Recipe can be made to this point several hours ahead.

COOKING Melt the butter in a skillet. Add the beans, season to taste with salt and pepper, and heat until warmed through, about 1 minute.

MAKES ❽ SERVINGS

LEMON CARROTS

*T*his quick and easy method of preparation produces carrots that are tender-crisp in texture, bright in color, and rich in natural flavor.

1 lemon
1 tablespoon chopped parsley
5 carrots
2 tablespoons butter
1 tablespoon sugar
Salt and ground black pepper

PREPARATION Grate zest from lemon. Squeeze juice. Chop parsley. Cut carrots on an angle into thin slices.

COOKING AND SERVING Melt butter in a large skillet over medium heat; add the carrots, $1/4$ cup water, and sugar. Cook, stirring as needed, until tender, about 7 minutes. Add lemon juice and toss to combine. Season with salt and pepper. Transfer carrots to a plate, sprinkle with parsley, and top with lemon zest.

MAKES 4 SERVINGS

Full-flavored kale is a highly underrated member of the cabbage family. It stands up well to herbed, spicy combinations, yet it is also delectable when simply cooked and tossed with butter, salt, and pepper.

³/₄ pounds kale, ribs removed
¹/₂ cup milk
¹/₄ cup heavy cream
1 clove garlic, crushed
¹/₄ cup fresh breadcrumbs, from
   crustless white bread
2 tablespoons unsalted butter
1 egg
1 egg yolk
Salt and ground black pepper
Sautéed Radishes (recipe follows)

COOKING AND SERVING Bring a large saucepan of salted water to a boil and blanch kale until tender, 8 to 10 minutes. Drain, plunge into cold water, and squeeze dry, removing as much water as possible. Mince and set aside. Heat oven to 350°F. Butter four ¹/₂-cup custard molds. Butter 4 pieces of foil to cover molds. In a large skillet over medium-high heat, melt butter. Add kale and cook, stirring occasionally, until all liquid has evaporated, 3 to 5 minutes. Remove from heat and set aside. In a bowl, combine egg, egg yolk, milk mixture, kale, and salt and pepper. Divide timbale mixture evenly among prepared molds and cover with prepared foil. Put molds in a water bath and bring water to a simmer on top of the stove. Transfer to preheated oven and bake until just firm, 20 to 25 minutes. Lift molds from water bath and unmold. Surround with Sautéed Radishes and serve.

MAKES **4** SERVINGS

T

SAUTEED RADISHES

his colorful and crisp combination with the peppery-sweet flavor of radishes, can be used as a garnish or as a light side dish.

1½ tablespoons unsalted butter
1 shallot, chopped
32 radishes, sliced thin
Salt and ground black pepper

COOKING AND SERVING In a large skillet over medium-high heat, melt butter. Add shallot and cook until soft, 3 to 4 minutes. Add radishes and cook, stirring constantly, until they are coated with butter and hot through, no longer than 2 minutes. Remove from heat, season with salt and pepper, and serve immediately. Radishes will lose their bright red color if overcooked or if not served at once.

MAKES GARNISH FOR 4 SERVINGS

Nutritious and flavorful lima beans are a good accompaniment for a glazed country ham.

2½ pounds fresh *or* frozen young
  lima beans (about 3½ pounds in
  the shell)
2 large cloves garlic
⅔ cup chopped parsley
7 ounces butter
Salt and ground black pepper
½ cup cornmeal

PREPARATION Boil the lima beans in salted water until tender, about 10 minutes for fresh and 5 minutes for frozen. Drain. Mince garlic. Chop parsley.

COOKING In a skillet, melt the butter until it begins to foam and turns a light nutty brown. Add the beans and garlic. Season with salt and pepper and sauté until warmed through. Add the cornmeal and parsley and toss to coat.

MAKES 12 SERVINGS

At their peak in high summer, most tomato varieties can be used interchangeably in this recipe.

10 large, ripe plum tomatoes,
    peeled, seeded
4 tablespoons unsalted butter
Salt and white pepper
1 cup heavy cream
4 teaspoons minced fresh basil,
    parsley, chervil, *or* a mixture

PREPARATION Cut tomatoes into thin strips.

COOKING AND SERVING Melt butter in a skillet over medium-high heat. Add tomato strips and sauté, tossing, until just cooked, 4 to 5 minutes. Season with salt and white pepper and remove strips. Add cream to skillet and simmer, until sauce thickens enough to coat a spoon, about 5 minutes. Add herbs and tomato strips. Heat, adjust seasonings to taste, and serve.

MAKES **4** SERVINGS

SAUTEED MUSHROOMS WITH GARLIC

🔏

Because mushrooms have such a high moisture content, they don't require the addition of liquid during cooking. The minced garlic provides a welcome zest to this very quick sauté.

3 cloves garlic

3 pounds wild *or* domestic
    mushrooms (12 cups quartered)

6 tablespoons butter

Salt and ground black pepper

PREPARATION Mince the garlic. Quarter the mushrooms.

COOKING Melt butter in a large skillet over medium heat and cook until foamy. Add garlic and cook 1 minute. Add mushrooms, season with salt and pepper, and cook over medium-low heat until tender, about 5 minutes.

MAKES **12** SERVINGS

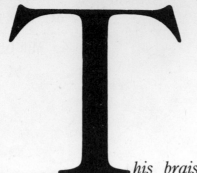

This braise, despite an unusual ingredient or two, has a traditional flavor. It goes well with roast turkey.

¼ pound baked ham
1 pound small to medium parsnips
4 tablespoons butter
1 cup chicken stock
½ cup orange juice
1 tablespoon light-brown sugar
Salt and ground black pepper

PREPARATION Trim the ham and cut it into ¼-inch dice. Peel and trim the parsnips.

COOKING Heat oven to 350°F. In a flameproof baking dish, melt the butter. Add the diced ham and cook over medium heat, stirring occasionally, until lightly browned, about 8 minutes. Add the stock, orange juice, brown sugar, and parsnips to the baking dish and cover tightly. Cook in preheated oven until the parsnips are tender, about 25 to 30 minutes. Transfer ham and parsnips to a warm serving dish. Bring the cooking liquid to a boil over high heat and cook, stirring often, until the liquid is slightly reduced, about 5 minutes. Pour the reduced liquid over the parsnips and season to taste with salt and pepper.

MAKES **4** SERVINGS

*Y*ou can use curly parsley or the stronger flavored flat-leaf parsley for these unusual fritters, which are at their best served warm and crisp.

8 cups loose packed parsley, stems removed (4 ounces)

4 egg yolks

¼ cup sour cream

2 tablespoons flour

Pinch nutmeg

Salt and ground black pepper

2 scallions, minced

2 tablespoons Parmesan cheese

2 egg whites

Oil for frying

PREPARATION Blanch parsley by putting it into a large pot of boiling water. As soon as water returns to a boil, stir, drain into a colander, and rinse with cold water. Squeeze out water and toss with your hands. In a large bowl, whisk together egg yolks, sour cream, flour, nutmeg, and salt and pepper. Add scallions, parsley, and cheese and stir. At this point, batter can be set aside, covered, for several hours before finishing. In another bowl, beat egg whites until they form stiff peaks. Using a spatula, thoroughly fold about ⅓ of the beaten whites into batter. Lightly fold in remaining whites. Do not overmix.

COOKING Heat ¼ inch of oil in a large skillet and then spoon in batter, using a heaping tablespoon for each fritter. Do not crowd pan. Fry about 30 seconds per side and then transfer to a warm plate lined with paper towels. Keep fritters warm until all batter is used.

MAKES **12** TWO-INCH FRITTERS

ASPARAGUS WITH COUNTRY HAM AND LEMON BUTTER

*H*ere the asparagus stalks are topped with country ham, sauced with lemon butter, and sprinkled with toasted almonds. Fully cooked smoked ham can also be used in this recipe.

24 asparagus spears

1 tablespoon olive oil

½ shallot, chopped

1 small clove garlic, minced

¼ cup vermouth

¼ cup lemon juice

¼ cup heavy cream

12 ounces unsalted butter, cut into small cubes, chilled

Salt and ground black pepper

Tabasco

2½ teaspoons grated lemon zest

¼ pound country ham, cut into julienne

1 tablespoon unsalted butter

¼ cup sliced blanched almonds, toasted

PREPARATION Break off bottom white/purple area of asparagus spears and discard. Carefully peel spears with a vegetable peeler, starting about 1 ½ inches from tip downward. Mince peelings and set aside.

COOKING *For the sauce,* heat olive oil in a saucepan. Sauté shallot, garlic, and minced asparagus trimmings for 1 to 2 minutes. Add vermouth and lemon juice and continue to cook until reduced by ²/₃. Add cream and reduce by ½. Lower heat and whisk in butter cubes, piece by piece, until sauce is smooth and all butter is incorporated. Remove from heat and season with salt and pepper and Tabasco. Strain and add lemon zest. Set aside in a warm place. Do not overheat or sauce will break. Cook asparagus in a covered steamer or in a saucepan of boiling, salted water to cover over high heat until just tender, about 5 minutes. Drain. In a skillet, sauté ham in 1 tablespoon butter over medium-high heat just until heated through.

SERVING Arrange asparagus on a warm serving plate, top with warm ham and lemon butter sauce. Sprinkle with toasted almonds. Serve immediately.

MAKES **4** SERVINGS

ASPARAGUS BUNDLES WITH CORNICHON VINAIGRETTE

A vinaigrette fortified with cream, egg yolks, and cornichons (small sour pickles) becomes a substantial and assertive sauce for pencil-thin asparagus.

Cornichon Vinaigrette
4 medium shallots
3 cornichons
1/2 cup olive oil
2 tablespoons rice-wine vinegar
2 tablespoons heavy cream
2 tablespoons Dijon mustard
2 egg yolks
Salt and ground black pepper

Asparagus Bundles
60 pencil (thin) asparagus (1 1/2
   pounds)
1 medium leek
Salt and ground black pepper

PREPARATION *For the vinaigrette*, peel and mince the shallots. Mince the cornichons. Whisk the next 5 ingredients together in a bowl, then whisk in shallots and cornichons. Season with 1/2 teaspoon salt and 1/4 teaspoon pepper and adjust seasoning to taste. (Can cover and refrigerate overnight.) *For the asparagus*, remove 1 inch from the stems; trim spears to the same length. Trim leek and carefully remove 3 leaves. Wrap and reserve remainder of the leek for another use.

COOKING Bring 2 inches of water to boil in a deep skillet. Add 2 teaspoons salt and the leek leaves and simmer until tender and bright green, about 2 minutes; drain on paper towels. Bring water back to a boil and cook asparagus in batches, simmering until tender, about 3 minutes. Refresh asparagus under cold running water; drain. (Can cover and refrigerate vegetables overnight.)

SERVING Cut leek leaves lengthwise into twelve 1/2-inch wide strips. Divide the asparagus into 12 bundles. Tie each asparagus bundle with a leek strip. Top asparagus bundles with vinaigrette and serve immediately.

MAKES **12** SERVINGS

espite its appearance, rabe is a member of the turnip, not the broccoli, family. This easily prepared combination is a classic Southern Italian dish. Although four pounds of broccoli rabe might seem excessive, this vegetable reduces in volume while cooking.

2 cloves garlic
4 pounds small broccoli rabe
Salt
6 tablespoons olive oil
1 teaspoon hot red-pepper flakes

PREPARATION Peel and thinly slice the garlic. Trim broccoli rabe and peel tough stems; cut into 3-inch pieces. Put into a large bowl with cold water to cover; set aside, 30 to 45 minutes. **COOKING** Bring 6 quarts of water to a boil in a large soup kettle. Drain the broccoli rabe; add it and 2 tablespoons salt to the kettle. Bring to a boil, partially cover, and simmer until just tender, about 5 minutes. Drain the broccoli rabe. (Can refresh, drain and refrigerate overnight.) Heat the oil in a large skillet. Add the garlic and red-pepper flakes; sauté until garlic softens and starts to color, about 1 minute. Add the rabe and sauté until hot, 2 to 3 minutes; adjust seasoning and serve immediately.

MAKES 8 SERVINGS

☙

L

ow in calories and rich in minerals, the popular and never-out-of-season eggplant gets a spicy Oriental flavoring in this Chinese-inspired preparation.

1 pound oriental eggplant

Oil for frying

1/4 cup minced scallion

1 1/4 teaspoons minced fresh ginger

1 tablespoon minced garlic

1/2 teaspoon hot chili paste

4 teaspoons soy sauce

2 teaspoons rice wine *or* Scotch

2 teaspoons sugar

1 tablespoon Chinese black vinegar
   or Worcestershire

3/4 teaspoon sesame oil

PREPARATION Cut eggplant into 3- by 1/2-inch strips.
COOKING Heat about 2 inches oil in a wok. Fry eggplant in 2 batches until tender, being careful not to overcrowd wok, about 2 1/2 minutes for each batch. Allow oil to reheat between batches. Set aside in a colander to drain. Discard all but 1 1/2 tablespoons oil. Reheat wok over high heat. Add 1 tablespoon scallion, ginger, and garlic and stir-fry for 10 seconds. Add chili paste and stir-fry for 5 seconds. Add soy sauce, wine, sugar, vinegar, and sesame oil and bring to a boil. Add eggplant and toss until thoroughly heated.
SERVING Arrange eggplant on a platter and sprinkle with remaining 3 tablespoons chopped scallion. Serve immediately.

MAKES **4** SERVINGS

CARROTS, PEPPERS, AND CABBAGE IN LETTUCE CUPS

A rainbow of vegetables can be spooned into lettuce cups, which are an attractive addition to a dinner plate and easy for guests to handle. The dressing is a sweet, sour, and hot combination of sugar, balsamic vinegar, and red-pepper flakes.

12 large Bibb lettuce leaves
1/8 small red cabbage
1/8 small green cabbage
4 medium scallions
1 medium red bell pepper
1 medium yellow bell pepper
4 medium carrots (1 pound)
2 tablespoons olive oil

Dressing
1 cup balsamic vinegar
1/4 cup sugar
1/8 teaspoon cayenne pepper
3/4 teaspoon hot red-pepper flakes
1 1/2 teaspoons paprika
Salt
1/2 cup snipped chives

PREPARATION Rinse and spin lettuce dry. Cut cabbage wedges into 1-inch dice. Thinly slice scallions. Stem, seed, and cut peppers into 1-inch dice. Peel and cut carrots diagonally into 1/4-inch slices.

COOKING Heat oil in a medium skillet. Sauté cabbage and scallions until slightly tender, about 3 minutes; transfer to a bowl. Bring 1 quart of water to boil in a large saucepan. Add peppers and carrots and simmer until slightly tender, about 1 minute. Drain and refresh vegetables; drain again. Add vegetables to the bowl; set aside. *For the dressing,* bring all ingredients, including 1 teaspoon salt, to a boil in a saucepan. Simmer until mixture reduces to 1/2 cup. Cool slightly; pour over vegetables. Cover and marinate overnight in the refrigerator. Adjust seasoning.

SERVING Arrange lettuce on a serving platter. Fill each leaf with 1/4 cup of the marinated vegetables. Sprinkle with chives and serve at room temperature.

MAKES **12** SERVINGS

B

riefly blanched until barely tender, the full-flavored brussels sprouts are finished in a mixture of olive oil and butter.

A touch of tarragon makes this a sprightly complement to game birds.

½ pound brussels sprouts

1 tablespoon olive oil

3 tablespoons butter

2 tablespoons chopped fresh tarragon leaves *or* other fresh herb

Salt and ground black pepper

COOKING AND SERVING In a saucepan of boiling, salted water, cook sprouts until almost tender, 3 to 4 minutes. Drain and chill in ice water. Slice sprouts into halves and pat dry. Just before serving, heat olive oil in a large frying pan. Add butter and, when it foams and turns nut-brown, add sprouts and toss. Cook over high heat, stirring occasionally, until sprouts are browned and tender, 3 to 4 minutes. Toss in tarragon. Season with salt and pepper.

MAKES 4 SERVINGS

Stir delicate walnut oil into the sautéed zucchini to embolden the walnut taste.

6 small zucchini (1½ pounds)
Salt
1 large garlic clove
2 tablespoons butter
½ cup walnuts (2 ounces)
1½ tablespoons walnut oil
Ground black pepper

PREPARATION Rinse and pat zucchini dry and trim off ends. Slice the zucchini into ¼-inch thick rounds with a sharp knife or the thin slicing disk of a food processor. Put zucchini in a colander and toss with 1 tablespoon salt. Let stand for 30 minutes, rinse, and pat dry. Peel and mince the garlic.

COOKING Heat butter in a large skillet. Add the walnuts and sauté over medium heat until golden and fragrant, about 3 minutes. Remove walnuts with a slotted spoon; set aside. Add the zucchini and garlic and sauté over medium-high heat, stirring constantly, until tender, about 5 minutes. Stir in the walnut oil and season with ¼ teaspoon pepper.

SERVING Transfer zucchini to a warmed serving dish, sprinkle with walnuts, and serve immediately.

MAKES **6** SERVINGS

Vegetagle Medley with Green-Pea and Mint Sauce

Vegetables cooked in the microwave have a more intense, fresher taste, more brilliant color, and need less salt.

3 carrots (¹/₂ pound)

¹/₂ pound young, tender green beans

8 brussels sprouts (¹/₂ pound)

2 heads Belgian endive

4 small turnips (³/₄ pound)

3 cups broccoli florets (1 pound)

2 yellow squash

1 cup oyster *or* other mushrooms (¹/₄ pound)

2 scallions

Green-Pea and Mint sauce (recipe follows)

2 teaspoons lemon juice

PREPARATION Cut carrots on an angle into ¹/₂-inch thick slices. Trim the beans. Trim the brussels sprouts and endives and cut in half lengthwise. Peel the turnips and cut into ¹/₂-inch wedges. Separate the broccoli tops into small florets. (You won't use the thick stem for this recipe.) Cut the squash on an angle into ¹/₂-inch thick pieces. Trim mushrooms and cut into ¹/₂-inch thick slices. Trim scallions and slice into ¹/₂-inch pieces. Around the edge of a 12-inch round microwaveable serving platter with 1-inch deep rim, alternate groups of carrots, green beans, turnips, and brussels sprouts. Make a ring of broccoli florets just inside the outer ring. For the final, innermost ring alternate the endive and yellow squash. Scatter the mushrooms and scallions over all.

COOKING AND SERVING Make the Green-Pea and Mint Sauce. Mix together ¹/₄ cup water and the lemon juice and pour over all the vegetables. Cover tightly with plastic wrap. Cook vegetables on high until tender, about 12 minutes. Serve vegetables with warm Green-Pea and Mint Sauce.

MAKES **4** SERVINGS

🌿

This flavorful sauce has the consistency of a thick mayonnaise. Try it also on chicken and fish.

1/2 pound shelled fresh or frozen
   green peas (1¼ pounds in shell)
1 tablespoon coarse salt
2 sprigs fresh mint
1 tablespoon lemon juice
1/2 cup olive oil
Ground black pepper

PREPARATION Shell peas if using fresh.
COOKING AND SERVING Put peas, 2 tablespoons water, and salt in a 1-quart glass measure and cover tighly with plastic wrap. Microwave on high until tender, 10 minutes for fresh, 3 minutes for frozen. Puree peas, mint, and lemon juice in a food processor until smooth. With machine running, add the olive oil in a slow, steady stream, and then add 1/2 cup of warm water in the same way. Season to taste with salt and pepper. Transfer to a bowl and serve with vegetables.

MAKES 2 CUPS

ggs have to be treated gently in the micro-wave oven. They easily overcook and turn rubbery. Additionally, the yolks need to be pricked with the tip of a knife so as not to explode.

Vegetable Medley (page 169)
4 eggs

PREPARATION Assemble Vegetable Medley and cover tightly with plastic wrap.

COOKING Cook in the microwave on high for 10 minutes. Remove from oven and uncover. Break each egg in turn into a cup and carefully slide onto vegetables where first and second ring meet. Pierce egg yolks with a pin or the tip of a small knife. Cover dish tightly with 2 sheets of plastic wrap, and cook on high until the eggs are just cooked and vegetables are very tender, about 2 minutes.

MAKES 4 SERVINGS

SALADS AND DRESSINGS

Bread Salad with
Onions
174

Spinach Salad with
Tomato-Shallot
Dressing
175

Creamy Coleslaw
176

Waldorf Salad
177

Arugula Salad
178

Cucumber and
Pepper Salad
179

Curried Chicken
Salad with Fresh
Basil
180

Mesclun Salad
181

Salami and Cheese
Salad
182

Tomato and
Mozzarella Salad
183

Summer Melon
Salad
184

Medley Salad with
Vinaigrette
185

Herb
Vinaigrette
186

Bulgur Garden
Salad
187

Seafood and Barley
Salad
188

Provençal Bean
Salad
189

Radish and Fennel
Salad
190

Salad of Dark
Greens, Radicchio,
and Shrimp
191

Warm Finnish
Potato Salad
192

Cucumber and Brie
Salad
193

S*weet summer onions, garden tomatoes,
fresh basil, and fruity olive oil make this Italian dish perfect for summer.
Good-quality bread is essential for the salad. Choose a flavorful, firm-
textured rustic loaf.*

Vinaigrette
1 clove garlic
3 tablespoons red wine vinegar
¹/₂ cup olive oil
Salt
1 clove garlic

**1 pound firm-textured bread (1
     standard loaf)**
Olive oil for brushing
¹/₂ sweet red bell pepper
3 tomatoes
¹/₂ onion
1 cup fresh basil leaves

PREPARATION *For the vinaigrette*, mince the garlic and combine in a bowl with the vinegar. Let sit for a few minutes. Whisk in the oil and season with salt to taste. Set aside. Heat oven to 350°F. Split the garlic clove. Remove crusts from bread, cut into approximately ³/₄-inch slices, and toast in preheated oven. While still warm, brush both sides of the bread with oil and then rub with garlic. Cool and cut into cubes. You should have about 4 cups. Dice the red peppers. Seed the tomatoes and chop into rough pieces about the same size as the bread cubes. Cut onion into thin slices. If basil leaves are small, leave them whole; otherwise, tear them into pieces. Toss together the bread cubes, basil, peppers, onion, and tomatoes, including their juice. (Recipe should be done to this point about ¹/₂ hour before serving.)

SERVING Pour ²/₃ to all the vinaigrette over the salad, depending on juiciness. Be careful not to oversoak the bread.

MAKES 4 SERVINGS

Spinach Salad with Tomato-Shallot Dressing

This healthy, light variation of the popular spinach salad is low in calories and free of cholesterol.

Spinach Salad

1/2 cucumber, peeled, cut lengthwise into thin slices, seeded, and then cut crosswise into 2 1/2-inch pieces
5 cups chiffonade of spinach
2 cups chiffonade of radicchio

Tomato-Shallot Dressing

1 tomato, peeled, seeded, and chopped
5 tablespoons white wine vinegar
4 teaspoons safflower oil
1 teaspoon salt
1 large shallot, minced

PREPARATION AND SERVING *For the salad,* crisp cucumber in ice water to cover for 4 hours. *For the dressing,* combine tomato, 3 tablespoons of the vinegar, oil, salt, and shallot in a food processor. Blend until smooth and set aside. To serve, toss spinach and radicchio in remaining 2 tablespoons vinegar. Spoon dressing on 4 chilled salad plates. Drain cucumber. Mound spinach-radicchio mixture in center of plates and top with drained cucumber.

MAKES 4 SERVINGS

*T*he cooked, slightly sweet dressing gives this coleslaw an old-fashioned character.

Cream Dressing

1 small garlic clove
1 teaspoon cornstarch
$1/3$ cup heavy cream
1 egg
1 tablespoon sugar
1 teaspoon honey
$3/4$ teaspoon dry mustard
2 tablespoons white wine vinegar
$1/2$ small lemon
2 teaspoons softened butter
$1/2$ teaspoon celery seed
$1/8$ teaspoon cayenne pepper
Salt and white pepper
$2/3$ cup mayonnaise

Vegetables

1 pound red cabbage
1 pound green cabbage
1 large onion
1 large green pepper

PREPARATION AND COOKING *For the dressing*, peel and mince garlic. Dissolve cornstarch in cream. Put egg, sugar, honey, and dry mustard in a nonreactive saucepan and whisk until smooth. Add the garlic, cream, and vinegar and whisk over low heat until mixture coats the back of a spoon, about 1 minute. Squeeze in $1/2$ teaspoon lemon juice. Whisk in butter, celery seed, cayenne pepper, $1/4$ teaspoon salt, and $1/4$ teaspoon white pepper. Strain dressing into a bowl and set aside to cool. Stir in mayonnaise. (Can refrigerate up to 2 days.) *For the vegetables*, remove the outer leaves from the cabbages. Shred cabbages ($4^{1}/2$ cups each) and transfer to a large bowl. Peel, halve, and thinly slice the onion. Cut green pepper into $1/4$-inch julienne strips. Add onion and pepper to the bowl and stir in dressing. Adjust seasoning.

MAKES 8 SERVINGS

T his now-traditional salad was conceived by Oscar of the Waldorf for the New York hotel's 1893 opening.

Walnut Oil Mayonnaise
1 egg
1 egg yolk
¼ teaspoon Dijon mustard
⅛ teaspoon curry powder
¾ teaspoon salt
1 tablespoon lemon juice
¼ cup walnut oil
¾ cup safflower oil
¼ cup heavy cream

Salad
1½ cups chopped walnuts
2 small heads Bibb *or* Boston
    lettuce
2 medium red delicious apples
2 medium Granny Smith apples
1 tablespoon each lemon juice and
    orange juice
4 medium celery stalks
2 tablespoons dried currants
3 tablespoons orange zest
Red seedless grapes, for garnish

PREPARATION In the workbowl of a food processor fitted with the metal blade, blend the first 6 ingredients for about 10 seconds. Add oils in a thin, steady stream with the machine running, about 60 seconds. Or, whisk all ingredients except oils and cream in a small bowl until smooth. Add oils in a slow, steady stream until smooth. Whip cream to soft peaks and fold into mayonnaise. (Can cover and refrigerate up to 3 days.) Preheat oven to 350°F and adjust oven rack to middle position. Spread walnuts on a baking sheet and toast until light brown, about 8 minutes. Wash, dry, and separate lettuce leaves. Core and cut apples into ½-inch dice. Toss apples with lemon and orange juices in a large bowl. Cut celery into ½-inch dice and add to the bowl along with the walnuts and currants. Toss mayonnaise with salad until thoroughly combined.

SERVING Place lettuce leaves on individual salad plates. Spoon a portion of salad onto the lettuce, sprinkle with grated orange zest, and garnish each plate with several grapes.

MAKES **8** SERVINGS

Arugula Salad

Arugula's dark green, jagged leaves are best when small, about four or five inches long.

5 ounces slab bacon, cut into bite-size pieces

2 eggs, lightly beaten

¼ cup cider vinegar

1 ½ teaspoons honey

Dash paprika

Salt and ground black pepper

½ cup milk

4 tablespoons unsalted butter

10 ounces arugula, chopped

PREPARATION AND SERVING In a small skillet over medium high heat, cook bacon until crisp and browned. Set aside with fat. In a small bowl, combine eggs, vinegar, honey, paprika, and salt and pepper. In a large saucepan over medium heat, warm milk. Remove from heat and add butter. When butter is melted, slowly add ½ of the milk/butter mixture to the egg mixture, whisking continuously, and then add this to remaining milk/butter in the pan. Cook gently, stirring constantly, over low to medium heat until just thickened, about 3 minutes. Do not overheat. Remove from heat and quickly add arugula, bacon, and bacon fat, tossing until well mixed. Serve immediately.

MAKES **4** SERVINGS

CUCUMBER AND PEPPER SALAD

*S*elect cucumbers that are dark green, firm, small and thin. Large, fat cucumbers may be bitter and have tough seeds.

2 cucumbers

3 plum tomatoes

1 green bell pepper

1 tablespoon fresh rosemary *or* 1 teaspoon dried

²/₃ cup olive oil

2 teaspoons mustard

3 tablespoons white wine vinegar

¼ teaspoon cayenne pepper *or* to taste

Salt and ground black pepper

PREPARATION Peel the cucumbers. Cut them in half lengthwise, seed, and then cut crosswise into thin half-moon-shaped slices. Peel, seed, and dice the tomatoes. Char the bell pepper over a gas flame, under the broiler, or on the grill until the skin is blistered. Peel, core, seed, and cut the pepper into thin strips. Chop the rosemary. Heat 2 table-spoons of the oil in a small frying pan over medium-high heat. Add the rosemary and cook until it just starts to turn golden, about 3 minutes. Remove pan from heat and add the remaining oil. In a bowl, whisk together the mustard, vine-gar, cayenne, and about ¹/₂ teaspoon salt. Gradually whisk in the rosemary and oil mixture. (Recipe can be made to this point a few hours ahead.)

SERVING Toss the cucumbers, tomatoes, and bell pepper with the dressing. Season to taste with salt and black pepper.

MAKES **4** SERVINGS

I

n this simple but subtle version of the classic chicken salad, the additions of curry for spice and basil for color and flavor result in a most pleasing combination. It can be served as is, or made into hearty sandwiches.

2 tablespoons oil

4 boneless chicken breasts

1 teaspoon curry powder

Salt and ground black pepper

Mayonnaise

1 egg yolk

2 teaspoons lemon juice

Salt and ground black pepper

1/2 cup oil

1 large tomato

1/3 cup chopped basil plus a small
    handful of leaves

8 slices hearty bread, such as
    cracked wheat, if making
    sandwiches

PREPARATION Heat the oil in a large skillet over medium-high heat. Sprinkle the chicken with curry powder, salt, and pepper and cook for 4 minutes. Turn, cover, and cook until browned and just cooked through, about 4 minutes more. Remove chicken from pan and let cool. Reserve pan juices. *For the mayonnaise*, scrape the reserved pan juices into a small bowl, add the egg yolk, and whisk in the lemon juice and 1/2 teaspoon salt. Whisk in the oil, drop by drop at first and then, when the sauce has emulsified, in a thin stream. Season to taste with salt and pepper. Cut the chicken into bite-size pieces and toss with the mayonnaise. (Recipe can be done to this point a few hours ahead.)

SERVING Slice the tomato. Chop 1/3 cup basil. Stir the chopped basil into the chicken salad and season to taste with salt and pepper. Put salad on a plate with the sliced tomato on the side and garnish with basil leaves. *Or*, toast bread and fill with curried chicken, tomato, and basil leaves.

MAKES **4** SERVINGS

*T*he name mesclun *derives from the Nicoise* word for mixture. The diversity of colors, flavors, and textures in mesclun *turns a simple green salad into a splendid dish that stands up to* assertive accompaniments.

1 clove garlic, crushed with a pinch of salt

2 shallots, cut into small dice

3 tablespoons red wine vinegar

Few drops balsamic vinegar *or* squeeze of lemon juice

½ cup fruity extra-virgin olive oil plus more if necessary

Salt and ground black pepper

1 handful each of 6 very young salad greens, such as red and green lettuces, curly endive, rocket, chervil, and green chicory

MAKES **6** SERVINGS

PREPARATION AND SERVING Combine garlic/salt mixture, shallots, red wine vinegar, and balsamic vinegar or lemon juice in bowl and let stand for a few minutes. In a slow, steady stream, add oil, whisking continuously. Season with pepper and more salt if necessary. Put greens into a large salad bowl, toss with just enough vinaigrette to coat them lightly, and serve immediately.

SALAMI AND CHEESE SALAD

H*ere is a virtually indestructible salad, perfect for packing into a picnic. Its greatest virtue, though, aside from requiring no cooking, is the speed with which it goes together.*

Balsamic and Mustard-Seed Dressing
¹/₃ cup balsamic vinegar
1 tablespoon yellow mustard seeds
³/₄ cup olive oil

4 scallions
2 red bell peppers
1 pound salami *or* other ready-to-eat spiced sausage
³/₄ pound Gruyère *or* cheddar cheese
5 ears corn *or* 2¹/₂ cups frozen kernels
Salt and ground black pepper
1 head romaine lettuce

PREPARATION *For the dressing,* stir together the vinegar and mustard seeds in a small bowl. Let stand for about 30 minutes. Whisk in the oil. Trim and cut the scallions, including green tops, into thin slices. Seed the peppers and cut them into ¹/₄-inch dice. Cut both the salami and cheese into ¹/₂-inch cubes. Cook corn in boiling, salted water until tender, about 5 minutes. Cool. Cut the kernels from the cobs. Or, cook frozen corn in a small amount of water. In a bowl, combine the scallions, peppers, salami, cheese, and corn and toss with dressing. Season to taste with salt and pepper. (Recipe can be made 1 day ahead.)

MAKES 4 SERVINGS

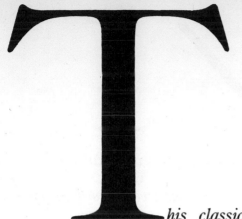

TOMATO AND MOZZARELLA SALAD

This classic combination of garden-ripe tomatoes and creamy mozzarella travels well to any summer picnic.

½ pound whole-milk mozzarella
½ red onion
2 small plum tomatoes
¼ cup finely shredded fresh basil
1 tablespoon red wine vinegar
1 tablespoon olive oil
Salt and coarse black pepper

PREPARATION Cut the mozzarella into 2-inch long, ¼-inch wide sticks. Mince the onion. Core, quarter, and seed the tomatoes and cut into thin wedges. Cut the basil crosswise into thin strips. Combine all the ingredients in a large bowl. Taste and add more salt and pepper as needed. Serve at room temperature or slightly chilled.

MAKES **4** SERVINGS

*U*se a number of different melons to give a variety of colors and flavors. Balance the sweetness with lemon juice, salt, and olive oil, then add mint or one of the more exotic basil varieties, and serve the salad chilled as a first course.

3 to 4 small melons
¼ cup extra-virgin olive oil
½ medium lemon
24 stemmed mint *or* basil leaves,
    plus 1 sprig for garnish

MAKES **8** CUPS

PREPARATION Seed and cut one-half of each melon into eighths. Slice the melon off the rind and cut enough 1-inch square chunks to measure 8 cups. Wrap and refrigerate remaining melon for another use. Put the melon into a bowl and toss with oil and ½ teaspoon salt. Squeeze in 1½ tablespoons lemon juice. (Can wrap and refrigerate overnight.) Julienne the mint and toss well with the melon.

MEDLEY SALAD WITH VINAIGRETTE

🖋

This simple salad is complemented by a classic vinaigrette. Make sure the greens are dry so the dressing adheres.

1½ quarts loosely packed greens, such as mâche, arugula, butter lettuce, *and/or* romaine

½ cup Vinaigrette (recipe follows)

PREPARATION Wash and thoroughly dry greens. Make the vinaigrette.

SERVING Gently toss the greens with the vinaigrette to coat. Season to taste.

MAKES **4** SERVINGS

You can use any kind of oil and vinegar in this dressing, and lemon juice can be substituted for the vinegar. Mustard added to the vinegar will aid in emulsification.

1 tablespoon minced fresh herbs such as parsley *and/or* chives
2 tablespoons wine vinegar
Salt and ground black pepper
6 tablespoons light oil, such as peanut

PREPARATION Mince the herbs. In a small bowl, whisk the vinegar and about ½ teaspoon salt until the salt dissolves. Gradually whisk in the oil. Add the herbs. Season to taste with salt, if needed, and pepper.

MAKES **1** CUP VINAIGRETTE

ulgur — also known as cracked wheat

—is a partially processed product that requires practically no cooking.

For this salad a jalapeño pepper adds bite to the vinaigrette dressing.

2½ teaspoons salt
2 cups bulgur
2 large red bell peppers
2 large ripe tomatoes
3 zucchini
4 scallions

Herb and Jalapeño Vinaigrette
1 jalapeño pepper
1 cup fresh coriander leaves
1 cup mint leaves
5 tablespoons white wine vinegar
Salt and ground black pepper
¾ cup olive oil
Salad greens, such as Romaine,
    arugula, watercress, or Bibb
½ pound sharp, white, crumbly
    cheese, such as feta or chèvre

PREPARATION In a small saucepan, bring 3 cups water to a boil. Stir in 2½ teaspoons salt and pour boiling water over bulgur in a bowl. Let stand, stirring once or twice, for 45 minutes. Strain bulgur, pressing with the back of a spoon to extract any water that hasn't been absorbed. Transfer bulgur to a mixing bowl. Roast peppers in flame of a gas burner or under a broiler until blackened. Peel, seed, and cut peppers into ½-inch dice. Halve the tomatoes, squeeze out seeds, cut into ½-inch dice. Cut zucchini into ½-inch dice. Slice the scallions. Toss bulgur with peppers, tomatoes, zucchini, and scallions. *For the vinaigrette*, stem and seed jalapeño. Pulse jalapeño, coriander, mint, vinegar, and ½ teaspoon salt in a food processor until smooth. With motor still running, slowly add oil. Pour dressing over bulgur and toss. Adjust seasoning with salt and pepper.

SERVING Line 4 plates with greens. Mound bulgur salad onto greens. Crumble cheese evenly over each salad.

MAKES **4** SERVINGS

T

his is a perfect salad for high summer —
cool and fresh tasting yet substantial enough to be the focus of a meal. To
make this salad when fresh basil is harder to come by, use dill or parsley
in the vinaigrette instead.

1¹/₃ cups pearl barley

³/₄ pound shrimp

³/₄ pound bay scallops

3 ribs celery

1 large red onion

10 black Mediterranean olives

Lemon and Basil Vinaigrette

1¹/₂ cups loosely packed basil
    leaves

2 tablespoons lemon juice

Salt and ground black pepper

²/₃ cup olive oil

Sprigs of basil for garnish (optional)

PREPARATION Bring a large pot salted water to a boil. Stir in barley, lower heat, and simmer, uncovered, stirring once or twice, until barley is tender, about 25 minutes. Drain and rinse with cold water. Put into a mixing bowl. Shell and devein shrimp and slice in half lengthwise. Trim scallops. Dice the celery and onion. Pit and chop the olives. Bring a pot of salted water to a boil. Add shrimp and scallops. After 1 minute (water does not have to return to a boil), drain seafood and cool to room temperature. Toss seafood with barley. Stir in celery and onion. *For the vinaigrette*, pulse basil, lemon juice, and ¹/₂ teaspoon salt in a food processor until almost smooth. Scrape the sides of the bowl. With motor running, slowly add oil. Pour dressing over the salad and toss well. Season to taste with salt and pepper and toss again.

SERVING Garnish salad with chopped olives and sprigs of basil, if desired. Serve cool or at room temperature.

MAKES **4** SERVINGS

Provençal Bean Salad

*T*he black olive puree for this salad is available at specialty stores. If unavailable, you can puree about four pitted black olives to make 1 tablespoon.

1 pound thin green beans
¼ cup black Mediterranean olives
¼ cup small green Mediterranean olives
12 radishes

Black-Olive Vinaigrette
1 tablespoon black olive puree
1½ tablespoon red wine vinegar
Salt and ground black pepper
¼ cup olive oil

PREPARATION Trim and wash the beans. Pit the olives. Slice the radishes. In a pot of salted, boiling water, cook the beans until just tender, 5 to 7 minutes. Drain and refresh under cold, running water. Drain thoroughly. *For the vinaigrette*, whisk together the olive puree, vinegar, and salt and pepper. Whisk in oil and taste for seasoning.

SERVING Toss beans, olives, and vinaigrette together. Put on plates and garnish with radishes. Serve at room temperature.

MAKES **4** SERVINGS

*F*reshly pulled at their peak, all spring radishes are sweet and crisp. With their green tops, they are a charming and colorful addition to a tossed green salad.

1 bunch radishes (about 12 medium
    or 24 very small radishes)
1 fennel bulb (about ¾ pound)
2 ounces Parmesan cheese
Salt and ground black pepper
½ cup olive oil
½ lemon
8 large sprigs flat-leaf parsley

PREPARATION Trim the root end from the radishes. Trim the fennel bulb. Cut both vegetables crosswise into thin slices. Set aside 12 of the radishes for garnish. Cut the cheese into very thin slices. Divide the fennel slices among 4 plates. Sprinkle with salt and pepper and drizzle with 3 tablespoons of the oil and a squeeze of lemon juice. Cover with a layer of fresh radish slices. Season with salt and pepper and drizzle with 3 more tablespoons oil and another squeeze of lemon juice. Scatter parsley sprigs over radishes, top with cheese slices, and drizzle with the remaining 2 tablespoons oil.

SERVING Garnish salads with the reserved radish slices and serve immediately with cracked black pepper.

MAKES **4** SERVINGS

T
SALAD OF DARK GREENS, RADICCHIO, AND SHRIMP

his party-sized recipe makes a delicious and colorful salad which will be a welcome addition to the buffet table.

Dressing

2 scallions

1 teaspoon grated fresh ginger

2 oranges

3 lemons

2 tablespoons whole-grain mustard

²/₃ cup white wine vinegar

Salt and ground black pepper

¹/₂ cup olive oil

1¹/₂ cups peanut oil

1 tablespoon sesame oil

¹/₂ cup parsley leaves

1 tablespoon cilantro leaves
    (optional)

1 pound snow peas

3 pounds large shrimp

1 large red onion

1 head bok choy

12 ounces spinach

2 heads romaine, 1 head escarole,
    and 1 head radicchio

PREPARATION *For the dressing,* chop scallions. Grate the ginger. Squeeze juices from oranges and lemons into the bowl of a food processor. Add the mustard, vinegar, ginger, scallions, and salt and pepper to taste and blend well. Gradually add the oils in a thin stream. Add the parsley and cilantro and blend until just smooth, with bits of the greens still visible. String the peas. Cook peas in boiling, salted water until they turn bright green, about 15 seconds. Plunge in cold water. Drain and dry. Using the same water, cook the shrimp until just opaque and slightly curled, about 2 minutes. Plunge in cold water and dry. Peel and devein the shrimp. Cut red onion into thin slices and rinse under cold, running water for a few minutes to lessen its sharpness. Wash and separate the stalks of bok choy and cut into ¹/₄-inch slices, including some of the dark greens. Toss together the peas, shrimp, onion, and bok choy. Chill until just before serving. Wash spinach, romaine, escarole, and radicchio. Dry, wrap in paper towels, put in plastic bags, and refrigerate.

SERVING Tear the greens. Toss all the ingredients with the dressing and put into a serving bowl or on a deep platter.

MAKES 30 SERVINGS

Yellow Finnish potatoes are among the most flavorful spuds. Their firm, buttery texture makes them ideal for potato salad. If they are not available, use regular boiling potatoes in their place. This salad goes well with ham or roasted pork.

4 yellow Finnish potatoes (about 1
    pound)
1 bunch arugula (about ¼ pound)

Balsamic Vinaigrette
4 teaspoons balsamic vinegar
Salt and coarse pepper
¼ cup olive oil

COOKING Put potatoes in a pot with cold, salted water to cover. Cover, bring to a simmer, and cook until the potatoes are done, about 30 minutes. Drain. Peel, quarter, and slice the potatoes. Meanwhile, wash and dry the arugula. *For the vinaigrette*, combine the vinegar and salt and pepper in a large bowl. Slowly add oil, whisking continuously. Toss the arugula in the viniagrette. Add the warm potato slices. Season to taste with salt and plenty of pepper.

MAKES 4 SERVINGS

CUCUMBER AND BRIE SALAD

This portable salad makes perfect picnic fare. It can be made the day before, but be sure to pack the salt and pepper because the seasoning can fade somewhat as the salad sits.

½ small red onion
4 teaspoons balsamic vinegar
½ teaspoon lemon juice
3 tablespoons oil
½ cup shelled peas, fresh *or* frozen
   (5 ounces unshelled)
½ savoy *or* Napa cabbage
1 small carrot
½ English cucumber
½ pound Brie
Salt and ground black pepper

PREPARATION Halve and cut the onion into thin slices. In a bowl, whisk the vinegar, lemon juice, and oil together, add the onion, and set aside. Shell the peas and cook in boiling, salted water until tender, about 5 minutes. Drain. Core the cabbage and cut into thin strips. If desired, score carrot with a channel knife to make a flower/star design when the carrot is cut. Slice the carrot into paper-thin rounds. Halve the cucumber lengthwise and slice very thin. Cut the Brie into small pieces. Toss the peas, cabbage, carrot, cucumber, and cheese with the dressing. Season to taste with salt and pepper. Serve at room temperature.

MAKES **4** SERVINGS

CAKES AND COOKIES

Peanut Butter
Cookies
196

Classic
Shortbread
197

Ginger
Shortbread
198

Orange Hazelnut
Brownies
199

Devil's
Food Cake
200

Creamy Chocolate
Frosting
201

Butterscotch
Pudding Cake
202

Brandied Espresso
Pudding Cake
203

Rum
Pudding Cake
204

Walnut Fudge
Pudding Cake
205

P

eanut butter was invented in 1890 by a St. Louis doctor who promoted it as a health food. It was love at first bite for most Americans. Just how big, how thick, how chewy, or how crisp these cookies should be is a matter for regional squabbling. Here is a delicious variation of this American classic.

PEANUT BUTTER COOKIES

4 tablespoons butter

³/₄ cup peanut butter

¹/₂ cup packed dark-brown sugar

1 cup vanilla sugar (see note below)

2 eggs

2¹/₄ cups flour

¹/₄ teaspoon salt

¹/₂ teaspoon baking soda

PREPARATION Cream together the butter, the peanut butter, the brown sugar, and the vanilla sugar. A food processor does this quickly. Beat the eggs and add. Sift the flour, salt, and baking soda and add ¹/₂ to peanut butter mixture. Pulse or mix until smooth. Add remaining half of ingredients and pulse or mix until smooth. If processor clogs, remove dough from container and stir in remaining flour with a wooden spoon. Divide dough into thirds and wrap tightly. Freeze for 15 minutes and then refrigerate the cookie dough for 30 minutes. Heat oven to 400°F. Line cookie sheets with parchment paper. Working quickly and with cool hands, make small balls of dough about 1 inch in diameter. Put the balls on sheets about 2 inches apart. Press cookies flat and make a grid pattern with a fork dipped in flour.

COOKING Bake in preheated oven until cookies are slightly browned around edges, 10 to 12 minutes. Remove parchment paper from pan with cookies on it. Repeat procedure with remaining dough. Remove the peanut butter cookies with a thin, flexible spatula.

NOTE Vanilla sugar is sugar in which vanilla beans have been stored. If vanilla sugar is unavailable, 1 cup plain granulated sugar plus 1 teaspoon vanilla extract can be substituted for it in this recipe.

MAKES **4** DOZEN COOKIES

CLASSIC SHORTBREAD
❧

*S*hortbread   is   quintessentially   British, more especially Scottish, and subsequently has made its way all over the globe.

½ pound room-temperature, lightly salted butter *or* unsalted butter plus ⅛ teaspoon salt

½ cup granulated, superfine, *or* confectioners' sugar

1 teaspoon vanilla extract

Few drops almond extract (no more than ⅛ teaspoon)

2 cups less 2 tablespoons all-purpose flour

¼ cup rice flour *or* cornstarch

Granulated sugar for sprinkling

PREPARATION Cream the butter with the sugar, vanilla, and almond extract until the mixture is pale and fluffy, at least 3 minutes. Whisk together the all-purpose flour and the rice flour. Blend the dry ingredients into the creamed mixture just until the flour is incorporated; don't overwork it. Divide the dough into 2 parts. Press each portion firmly into a 9- or 10-inch pie pan and smooth the top. With a spatula, draw the edge of each dough round in from the sides of the pan, leaving ¼ inch of clear space. Pinch or crimp edges of the round. If the dough is very soft, you may want to chill it. Mark each round into 8 wedges with a knife, cutting the dough only halfway through. Chill the dough again for 30 minutes if it is soft. Prick each wedge all the way through in 2 to 3 places with a fork. Sprinkle shortbread lightly with sugar.

COOKING Heat oven to 325°F. Bake shortbread in center of preheated oven until creamy golden but not browned and center is firm to the touch, 25 to 30 minutes. If the shortbread is turning golden too quickly, cover pan loosely with foil and continue baking until shortbread is firm. Cool in pans, set on a rack, for 10 minutes. Cut the scored lines through and leave the pieces in the pan until almost cool. Transfer to a rack to cool completely.

MAKES 16 WEDGES

T hese gingery wedges are a delightful varia-
tion of the basic shortcake mixture which even the staunchest tradi-
tionalist will find pleasing.

**3 tablespoons minced candied
ginger plus slivers for decorating**
**Classic Shortbread (recipe
precedes)**
³/₄ teaspoon ground dried ginger

PREPARATION Mince the 3 tablespoons candied ginger. Follow Classic Shortbread recipe but omit the almond extract. Add minced candied ginger and dried ginger with the dry ingredients.

COOKING Shape and bake as instructed. Decorate with slivers of candied ginger before baking.

MAKES 16 WEDGES

ORANGE HAZELNUT BROWNIES

*T*he recipe for these brownies gives instruc-
tions for baking in conventional, convection, and microwave ovens.

Brownies

4 ounces unsalted butter, cut into
    pieces

2 ounces unsweetened chocolate,
    cut into pieces

2 eggs

³/₄ cup sugar

1 teaspoon vanilla extract

¹/₂ cup flour

¹/₂ teaspoon baking powder

¹/₈ teaspoon salt

2 teaspoons grated orange zest

¹/₂ cup hazelnuts, lightly toasted,
    skinned, and chopped

Grand Marnier Ganache Icing

¹/₂ cup heavy cream

3 ounces bittersweet chocolate,
    chopped

3 ounces semisweet chocolate,
    chopped

2 tablespoons unsalted butter,
    softened

¹/₄ teaspoon vanilla extract

1 tablespoon Grand Marnier

PREPARATION Heat conventional oven to 350°F. Heat convection oven to 325°F. If using conventional or convection oven, butter a 9- by 9-inch square baking pan. If using microwave oven, butter a glass, 9-inch round pie pan.

COOKING *For the brownies,* for microwave oven, put butter and chocolate into the glass dish and cook on medium power until melted, about 4 minutes. The chocolate will retain its shape even when melted, so you should stir a few times during melting. If using a conventional or convection oven, melt butter and chocolate in top of a double boiler, over hot water on low heat. For both methods, cool melted chocolate mixture about 5 minutes.

In a mixing bowl, lightly whisk eggs. Whisk in sugar and vanilla until thick. Sift together dry ingredients. Add chocolate mixture, flour mixture, and orange zest to egg mixture, beating until smooth. Stir in nuts and mix until well blended. Pour batter into prepared pan.

If using a conventional oven, bake in preheated oven until center is just set and firm, 25 minutes. If using convection oven, bake in a preheated oven for 15 to 18 minutes. If using microwave oven, bake on medium-high power, a total of 8 minutes, rotating dish. (Brownies cooked in the microwave will be moist in center.)

For the icing, scald cream in a heavy saucepan. Remove from heat and add chocolates all at once. Stir until chocolate is melted and smooth. Set aside for about 2 minutes. Add butter, vanilla, and Grand Marnier. Stir gently until mixture is smooth. Chill, covered, stirring occasionally, until thick enough to spread, about 1 hour. Frost brownies and chill until icing is firm, about 1 hour.

SERVING To serve, cut conventional and convection brownies into 12 squares. Cut microwave brownies into 12 wedges.

MAKES 12 SERVINGS

DEVIL'S FOOD CAKE

This is a dense, one-layer version of the classic American cake, with a creamy, chocolate frosting. It is good enough to eat unfrosted, if you increase the sugar called for in the recipe by a couple of tablespoons.

½ cup sugar

1 cup flour

½ cup lightly packed cocoa

1 teaspoon baking powder

1 teaspoon baking soda

½ teaspoon salt

4 tablespoons unsalted butter

1 cup boiling water

2 eggs

1 teaspoon vanilla extract

1 teaspoon red food coloring
   (optional)

Creamy Chocolate Frosting (recipe
   follows)

PREPARATION Heat the oven to 350°F. Butter an 8- or 9-inch cake pan. If using an ordinary pan, fit it with a round of parchment paper, and then butter again. Sift the sugar, flour, cocoa, baking powder, baking soda, and salt into a mixing bowl. Cut the butter into 6 pieces and put into a well in center of flour. Pour boiling water on top and stir gently until butter melts. Stir until blended and then beat until smooth. Lightly beat the eggs and add with vanilla and optional food coloring. Beat briefly with an electric mixer or about 50 strokes with a wooden spoon. Pour batter into prepared cake pan. Holding sides of the pan with your palms, strike it gently on the counter to settle the batter.

COOKING Bake in preheated oven until cake springs back when touched lightly, about 35 minutes. Remove from oven and let cake rest in pan for about 5 minutes. Turn cake out onto a rack and then invert so that right side is up. When cool, frost with Creamy Chocolate Frosting, swirling on the frosting with a rubber spatula.

SERVING Cut into wedges and serve.

MAKES ❶ NINE-INCH CAKE

CREAMY CHOCOLATE FROSTING

T his glossy, creamy frosting sets well but never gets hard. Its taste and texture, like that of the cake, are best at room temperature. If the cake must be refrigerated, allow 1 hour for it to return to room temperature.

2 ounces semisweet chocolate
2 tablespoons butter
1 egg yolk
½ cup sifted confectioners' sugar
Pinch salt
1 to 2 tablespoons heavy cream

PREPARATION Break up the chocolate.

COOKING In the top of a deep, narrow double boiler, melt chocolate and butter over very low heat. Using a wire whisk or electric beater, beat chocolate/butter mixture until smooth. Beat in egg yolk, confectioners' sugar, and salt. Add a bit of cream from time to time if frosting seems too dry. It should be creamy and easy to spread.

MAKES ENOUGH FROSTING FOR 1 NINE-INCH CAKE

*P*udding cake transforms itself in the oven from a thick batter to a fluffy sponge cake with its own rich, custardy sauce. Pecans are a natural with the butterscotch flavor.

²/₃ cup packed light-brown sugar

¹/₃ cup granulated sugar

3 tablespoons flour

¹/₄ teaspoon salt

2 eggs, separated

¹/₂ teaspoon vanilla

¹/₈ teaspoon grated lemon zest

1 cup milk

3 tablespoons unsalted butter, melted and cooled

¹/₃ cup lightly toasted chopped pecans

PREPARATION Heat oven to 350°F. In a mixing bowl, combine both sugars, flour, and salt. In another bowl, beat egg yolks. Stir into sugar mixture with vanilla, lemon zest, milk, and butter, combining well. In a third bowl, beat egg whites to stiff but not dry peaks. Carefully but thoroughly fold egg whites and pecans into batter. Pour into an unbuttered 1-quart baking dish and place in a larger pan containing about 1 inch of hot water.

COOKING Bake in preheated oven until set and top is well browned, 40 to 45 minutes.

MAKES **4** SERVINGS

T

BRANDIED ESPRESSO PUDDING CAKE

This dessert is best served warm and topped with whipped cream. If you can't find instant espresso in your local market, regular instant coffee may be used instead.

1 cup flour

1½ teaspoons baking powder

½ teaspoon baking soda

1½ cups granulated sugar

¼ teaspoon salt

2 tablespoons plus 1 teaspoon instant espresso

¼ cup milk

¼ cup heavy cream

3 tablespoons unsalted butter, melted and cooled

1 teaspoon vanilla

¼ cup packed light-brown sugar

1¼ cups very hot water

2 tablespoons brandy

Whipped cream (optional)

PREPARATION Heat oven to 350°F. In a mixing bowl, sift together flour, baking powder, baking soda, ¾ cup of the sugar, the salt, and 2 tablespoons of the espresso. In another bowl, combine milk, cream, butter, and vanilla. Stir into dry mixture until well blended. Spread in an unbuttered 8-inch baking pan. Combine brown sugar, remaining ¾ cup granulated sugar, and 1 teaspoon espresso. Sprinkle over batter. Combine hot water and brandy and pour over batter.

COOKING Bake in preheated oven until set and bubbly, 35 to 40 minutes. Serve with optional whipped cream.

MAKES 8 SERVINGS

*Y*ou can vary the taste of this easy to make dessert with your choice of spirits. In place of rum — either the dark or light variety — try using brandy or cognac.

1 cup sugar
3 tablespoons flour
¼ teaspoon salt
2 eggs, separated
1 cup milk
¼ cup rum
⅛ teaspoon nutmeg

PREPARATION Heat oven to 350°F. In a mixing bowl, sift together sugar, flour, and salt. In another bowl, beat egg yolks and add with milk, rum, and nutmeg to dry ingredients. In a third bowl, beat egg whites until stiff but not dry and carefully fold into batter. Pour into an unbuttered 1-quart baking dish and place in a larger pan containing about 1 inch of hot water. Bake in preheated oven until set and top is browned, 40 to 45 minutes.

MAKES ❹ SERVINGS

T his pudding cake makes a warming, home-style conclusion to a hearty meal. In this recipe, you can use the darker, more mellow-flavored Dutch processed cocoa, which has some of its natural acidity removed.

1 cup flour
2 teaspoons baking powder
1/4 teaspoon salt
1 cup granulated sugar
1/8 teaspoon ground cinnamon
6 1/2 tablespoons cocoa
1/4 cup milk
1/4 cup heavy cream
4 tablespoons unsalted butter, melted and cooled
1 teaspoon vanilla
1 cup chopped walnuts
3/4 cup dark-brown sugar, packed
1 3/4 cups very hot water
Whipped cream (optional)

MAKES 8 SERVINGS

PREPARATION Heat oven to 350°F. In a mixing bowl, sift together flour, baking powder, salt, 3/4 cup of the sugar, cinnamon, and 2 1/2 tablespoons of the cocoa. In another bowl, combine milk, cream, butter, and vanilla and then stir into dry mixture. Blend in walnuts. Batter will be stiff. Spread in an unbuttered baking pan. Combine brown sugar, remaining 1/4 cup granulated sugar, and 1/4 cup cocoa in a small bowl. Sprinkle over batter and pour hot water over it.

COOKING Bake in preheated oven until set and top is bubbly, 35 to 40 minutes. Serve warm with optional whipped cream.

DESSERTS

Peaches and White
Wine Ice
208

Peaches in Hot-
Buttered Rum
209

Peach Crepes
210

Nectarines Poached
in Port
211

Nectarines and
Plums with
Parmesan
212

Apricots with
Amaretti
213

Pears with
Mascarpone
214

Pears Stuffed with
Gorgonzola
215

Poached Pears with
Kirsch Sabayon
216

Baked Pears with
Shredded Chocolate
217

Icy Oranges with
Cinnamon
218

Blood Oranges with
Nutmeg
219

Almond- and
Cheese-Stuffed Figs
220

Figs with
Mascarpone
221

Tropical Fruit Salad
with Pecans and
Campari
222

Grilled Fresh
Pineapple
223

Riesling-Marinated
Strawberries
224

Minted
Strawberries
225

Mixed Fruit Platter
226

Melon in Port with
Coriander Cream
227

Clove-Studded
Apples
228

Fritters with
Cinnamon Wine
Sauce
229

Banana Fritters
230

White Chocolate
Mousse
231

Marbleized Pan
Souffle
232

Maple-Walnut
Zabaglione
233

M

uch of the preparation for this cool, sum-

mery dessert can be done ahead. All that is needed at serving time is a

quick assembly of the peaches and ice, and a garnish of fresh mint.

White-Wine Ice

1 lemon

3 cups fruity white wine

1 cup sugar

2 whole cloves

Poached Peaches

1 lemon

1 cup sugar

2 large peaches

2 cloves

Mint sprigs for garnish (optional)

PREPARATION *For the White-Wine Ice*, remove 1 strip zest from lemon, about 2 inches by $1/2$ inch. Squeeze 2 tablespoons juice. In a large, nonreactive saucepan, combine the wine, 1 cup of water, sugar, lemon juice, lemon zest, and cloves and bring to a boil. Simmer until the sugar dissolves, about 5 minutes. Strain into a container. Freeze in an ice-cream machine according to manufacturer's instructions or in the refrigerator freezer, stirring occasionally.

For the Poached Peaches, remove one 2-inch strip zest from lemon. Squeeze 2 tablespoons juice. In a small, nonreactive saucepan, bring 2 cups of water and the sugar to a simmer and cook until the sugar dissolves. Skin, halve, and pit the peaches. Add the lemon juice, lemon zest, cloves, and peach halves to the sugar syrup and poach over low heat for 5 minutes. Cool the peaches in their poaching liquid. Cover and chill. Recipe can be made to this point 1 day ahead.

SERVING Serve White-Wine Ice with peach halves and garnish with mint sprigs if you like.

MAKES **4** SERVINGS

PEACHES IN HOT-BUTTERED RUM

These rum-flavored peaches are delicious on their own or served warm over vanilla ice cream, lemony pound cake slices, or a simple custard.

1 large orange
4 large peaches
3 tablespoons butter
$1/4$ to $1/2$ cup dark-brown sugar
$1/4$ cup dark rum
1 tablespoon lemon juice
$1/4$ teaspoon ground cinnamon
$1/4$ teaspoon ground allspice

PREPARATION Use a zesting tool to remove 1 tablespoon of fine shreds of zest from the orange or cut off strips and then cut them crosswise into thin shreds. Squeeze 2 tablespoons orange juice.

COOKING AND SERVING Peel, pit, and cut the peaches into thin slices. Melt the butter in a large, nonreactive frying pan. Add the sugar and stir until dissolved, about 2 minutes. Add the rum, orange zest, and orange and lemon juices, and stir to combine. Put the peach slices in the pan and cook over low heat, basting with the sauce, until heated through, about 3 minutes. Transfer peaches to serving plates. Stir the cinnamon and allspice into the sauce and cook until reduced slightly, about 1 minute. Pour sauce over the peaches and serve immediately.

MAKES 4 SERVINGS

T

he reduced sugar, fat, and cholesterol in this recipe in no way compromise its flavor.

Crepes

2 egg whites

¹/₂ cup unbleached flour

¹/₂ cup plus 2 tablespoons skim milk

1 teaspoon baking powder

1¹/₂ teaspoons vegetable oil

Peach filling

1¹/₂ cups peeled, chopped peaches

¹/₄ cup raisins

¹/₄ teaspoon cinnamon

¹/₂ teaspoon lemon juice

4¹/₂ teaspoons orange juice

1 tablespoon skim milk

¹/₈ teaspoon cinnamon, combined with ¹/₈ teaspoon sugar

Mint leaves for garnish

PREPARATION *For the crepes*, combine egg whites, flour, milk, baking powder, and oil in a bowl with a whisk.

COOKING Heat a small frying pan or crêpe pan. Coat lightly with oil. Pour 2 tablespoons batter into pan. Slide batter around to distribute evenly. Cook over medium heat until crêpe is set, about 1 minute. Slide crêpe from pan, done side down. Repeat with remaining batter to make a total of 8 crêpes, using additional oil if necessary. Heat oven to 350°F. Oil a baking dish.

For the filling, simmer peaches, raisins, cinnamon, and lemon and orange juice until peaches are just tender, 8 minutes. Reserve ¹/₄ cup of the filling; put equal amounts of the remaining mixture in center of each crêpe. Roll or fold crêpe into thirds, handling very gently. Arrange crêpes so they do not touch in prepared pan. Using a pastry brush, brush crêpes with skim milk. Bake in preheated oven until just heated through, 5 to 8 minutes.

SERVING Remove crêpes from oven and sprinkle with cinnamon-sugar mixture. Top each crêpe with a tablespoon of reserved peach filling. Garnish with mint leaves.

MAKES ❹ SERVINGS

oaching in port adds depth and complexity to sweet juicy nectarines or peaches in this luscious, make-ahead combination with its interesting touch of spirits and spice.

3 oranges

1 lemon

2½ cups sugar

¾ cup port

3 whole cloves

1 one-inch piece cinnamon stick

¼ teaspoon grated nutmeg

3 pounds small nectarines,
   unpeeled

PREPARATION Remove 2 strips zest, about ½ inch by 2 inches each, from one of the oranges. Squeeze ½ cup orange juice. Remove 1 strip zest from lemon. Squeeze 3 tablespoons lemon juice. In a large, nonreactive saucepan, bring the sugar and 1½ cups water to a simmer and cook until sugar is dissolved, about 5 minutes. Add the orange and lemon juices and strips of zest, port, cloves, cinnamon stick, and nutmeg. Return liquid just to a boil. Add the whole nectarines and more water if necessary to just cover them. Poach over low heat for 5 minutes. Cool the nectarines in their poaching liquid for about 1 hour. With a slotted spoon, carefully transfer the nectarines to a separate container. Bring the poaching liquid to a boil and cook until it is thick and reduced by approximately one-third, about 30 minutes. Pour the thickened liquid over the nectarines and cool. Refrigerate for several hours.

SERVING Serve nectarines whole with their liquid poured over them.

MAKES **4** SERVINGS

A simple pairing of fresh fruit and red wine

becomes even more tasteful when complemented by slices of Parmesan.

¹/₄ pound Parmesan

2 nectarines

2 plums

4 teaspoons sugar

¹/₄ cup dry red wine

PREPARATION AND SERVING Cut Parmesan into 4 thin slices. Pit and slice nectarines and plums. Toss them with the sugar and wine. Serve the fruit with Parmesan on the side.

MAKES **4** SERVINGS

APRICOTS WITH AMARETTI

*A*maretti, the almond-flavored Italian macaroons, make this simple but elegant dessert a perfect ending to a summer meal.

3 tablespoons sugar

6 fresh apricots

2 tablespoons softened butter

1/3 cup Amaretti (Italian macaroon) crumbs

1/2 cup heavy cream

PREPARATION Generously butter a large baking dish or gratin dish and sprinkle with 1 tablespoon of the sugar. Halve and pit apricots. Arrange apricots in dish, cut sides up. Fill cavities of apricots with the softened butter and sprinkle with remaining 2 tablespoons sugar. Sprinkle Amaretti crumbs over fruit.

COOKING AND SERVING Heat broiler. Put baking dish under preheated broiler and cook until topping is bubbly and brown, about 5 minutes, watching carefully to make sure it doesn't burn. Serve warm with cold heavy cream.

MAKES **4** SERVINGS

PEARS WITH MASCARPONE

As an alternative to mascarpone, process 12 ounces of ricotta cheese with 1/4 cup light cream.

3/4 pound mascarpone or cream cheese

1/4 cup hazelnut- or walnut-flavored liqueur

3 tablespoons minced mint

1 medium lemon

6 medium Anjou or Bartlett pears (3 pounds)

12 walnut halves

6 mint springs

PREPARATION Beat the mascarpone cheese, liqueur, and mint until smooth. Halve the lemon and squeeze the juice into 4 quarts of cold water, then add the squeezed lemon halves. Peel, halve, stem, and core the pears and put them in the lemon water. (Can refrigerate up to 3 hours.)

SERVING Drain and arrange the pear halves on a platter or dessert plates. Top each pear half with 2 tablespoons of cheese mixture. Garnish with walnut halves and a mint sprig.

MAKES 4 SERVINGS

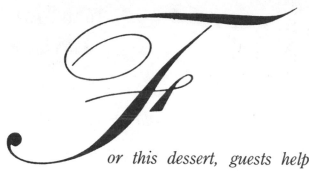

PEARS STUFFED WITH GORGONZOLA

*F*or this dessert, guests help themselves to pears and crack their own walnuts as desired. You might want to pass the port, too, as a perfect accompaniment to this dish.

4 to 6 pears
1 lemon
6 ounces Gorgonzola or other blue
cheese, at room temperature
1 pound whole walnuts, in the shell

PREPARATION AND SERVING Peel pears and halve lengthwise. Remove cores with a melon baller, making about a 1-inch cavity in each half. Squeeze lemon juice over pears to keep from darkening. Fill the cavities of each pear half with the softened cheese, and cut each filled pear in half again. Arrange pear wedges on a platter and serve with whole walnuts.

MAKES 4 SERVINGS

K irsch replaces the traditional Marsala in this cherry-flavored sabayon. Peaches are a fine substitute for pears.

Pears

3 tablespoons lemon juice
4 bartlett, bosc *or* seckel pears
1 cup sugar
1 cinnamon stick (2 inches long)

Sabayon

4 egg yolks
½ cup sugar
Salt
1 teaspoon vanilla
½ cup Spätlese *or* late harvest
    Riesling
2 tablespoons kirsch
⅓ cup sliced, toasted almonds

PREPARATION Dip a small melon baller in lemon juice and use it to core the pears from the blossom ends. Trim a thin slice off the blossom end of each pear so it sits flat. Peel pears, leaving stems on, and rub 2 tablespoons of lemon juice over an exposed surfaces to prevent discoloration.

COOKING *For the pears*, in a 3-quart saucepan, mix 4 cups of water, the sugar, and 1 tablespoon lemon juice. Bring to a simmer and add the cinnamon stick. Add pears to the syrup, making sure they are completely immersed. Simmer gently until a skewer easily pierces the pears, about 20 to 25 minutes. Remove from heat and cool pears in syrup. (Can cover and refrigerate up to one week.)

For the sabayon, mix egg yolks, sugar, salt, and vanilla in a large saucepan. Whisk until a heavy ribbon is formed. Put pan over low heat and gradually add the wine, whisking constantly, until sauce is frothy and thick enough to leave a trail when dripped from the whisk, 8 to 10 minutes. Whisk in the kirsch and remove from heat. (Can keep sauce warm without it separating for about 30 minutes.)

MAKES 4 SERVINGS

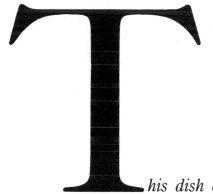

This dish can be served warm or chilled.
Shave the chocolate from a bar using either a knife or a swivel vegetable
peeler. You'll get more attractive shards of chocolate if you warm the bar
slightly in your hands first.

1 cup water
1 cup sugar
4 ripe pears
¼ pound semisweet chocolate

PREPARATION Put the water and sugar in a saucepan and bring to
a simmer. Cook until the syrup thickens slightly, about 8
minutes. Meanwhile, butter a shallow baking dish. Peel,
halve, and core the pears. Put the pears cut side down in the
prepared baking dish and pour syrup over them. Heat oven
to 350°F. Bake pears in preheated oven, turning once halfway through and basting occasionally, until tender, about 20
minutes.

SERVING Transfer pears to plates. Shave chocolate directly
over the pears while still warm. Serve warm or chilled.

MAKES ❹ SERVINGS

T*he luscious berries are a rich nutritional package. But they are highly perishable, and should be used as soon as possible for optimal flavor and texture.*

20 large strawberries
1½ cups chilled late-harvest
   Riesling *or* other sweet wine

PREPARATION Arrange strawberries in a shallow serving bowl or in individual bowls and pour wine over them. Refrigerate for about 30 minutes before serving.

MAKES **4** SERVINGS

Minted Strawberries and Sour Cream
§

ake advantage of the strawberry season with this delightful layering of berries and minty sour cream.

¾ cup sour cream

2 tablespoons sugar plus more for sprinkling

2 pints strawberries

3 tablespoons chiffonade of fresh mint plus a few leaves for garnish, if desired

PREPARATION Whisk the sour cream and 2 tablespoons sugar together. Hull and slice the strawberries.

SERVING Cut the mint leaves into thin strips. Stir the mint into the sourcream mixture. Divide ½ of the strawberries among 4 serving dishes, such as parfait glasses, and top each with a large spoonful of the sour-cream mixture. Top with remaining strawberries and then the cream mixture. Sprinkle with sugar to taste and garnish each serving with a mint leaf if desired.

MAKES **4** SERVINGS

T his dish looks especially pretty when made with a combination of red-skinned apples, such as Rome or Empire, and green-skinned, such as Granny Smith.

3 tablespoons butter

3 tablespoons dark-brown sugar

3 large apples

8 cloves, approximately

2 tablespoons lemon juice

1 teaspoon vanilla extract

1/2 cup heavy cream *or* crème fraiche

COOKING AND SERVING Heat oven to 350°F. Melt butter. Brush a large baking pan or gratin dish with some of the melted butter and sprinkle with about 1 tablespoon of the sugar. Core apples and slice into twelve 1/2-inch thick rounds. Arrange apple slices in the dish, overlapping, in 4 individual portions and stud with whole cloves. Combine lemon juice and vanilla. Sprinkle lemon juice and vanilla and then remaining 2 tablespoons sugar over the apples. Drizzle with remaining melted butter. Bake in preheated oven until just soft, about 15 minutes. Turn broiler on, put under broiler, and cook until top is dark brown, bubbly, and caramelized, about 2 minutes. Serve warm with cold cream.

MAKES 4 SERVINGS

FRITTERS WITH CINNAMON WINE SAUCE

These deep-fried pastry fritters, served with a clove, cinnamon, and honey-infused sauce, are of Spanish origin. The sauce may be prepared several days in advance, but the fritters should be fried shortly before serving.

Cinnamon Wine Sauce
¾ cup sugar
1 clove
1 whole allspice
1 cinnamon stick (2 inches long)
¼ cup red wine

Fritter Batter
4 tablespoons butter
⅔ cup all-purpose flour
3 large eggs

3 cups corn oil

PREPARATION AND COOKING *For the Cinnamon Wine Sauce,* put the sugar, clove, allspice, cinnamon, wine, and 2 cups of water in a medium saucepan. Bring liquid to a boil, stirring to dissolve sugar. Reduce heat to low and simmer until mixture thickens slightly, 15 to 20 minutes. Strain. (Can cover and refrigerate up to 2 weeks.)

For the fritters, cut the butter into small pieces. Bring ½ cup water to a boil with the butter in a medium saucepan. Remove saucepan from heat, add the flour all at once, and beat vigorously with a wooden spoon to form a paste. Cool for 3 minutes. Beat in eggs, one at time, thoroughly incorporating each egg before adding the next.

Heat the corn oil in a wok or deep skillet to 375°F. Working in batches, drop rounded tablespoons of dough into the oil and fry until golden brown, about 1½ minutes on each side. Drain on paper towels. (Can keep fritters warm in a 250°F oven up to 30 minutes.)

SERVING Warm the sauce in a saucepan. Transfer dumplings to bowls and top with warm sauce. Serve immediately.

MAKES 18 FRITTERS

BANANA FRITTERS

F *or best results, fritter batter should rest to let the gluten relax before dipping and frying.*

3 bananas, each cut into 6 pieces

3 tablespoons Grand Marnier

3 teaspoons sugar

²/₃ cup flour

¼ teaspoon salt

1 egg, separated

1 tablespoon butter, melted

⅓ cup orange juice

Zest of 1 orange, minced

Vegetable oil for deep-frying

Confectioners' sugar

PREPARATION In a small bowl, gently toss banana pieces, $1^1/_2$ tablespoons of the Grand Marnier, and $1^1/_2$ teaspoons of the sugar. In a large bowl, combine flour and salt. In a small bowl, combine egg yolk, butter, remaining $1^1/_2$ tablespoons Grand Marnier, remaining $1^1/_2$ teaspoons sugar, orange juice, and orange zest. Whisk egg mixture into flour just until thoroughly combined. Set aside for 30 minutes. In another bowl, beat egg white until stiff. Fold into batter. Add bananas with any accumulated juice.

COOKING In a pan or deep-fryer, heat oil to 375°F. Drop batter-coated bananas into hot oil, a few at a time. Brown on both sides, 3 to 5 minutes in all. Allow oil to return to 375°F before adding next batch. Drain on paper towels, sprinkle with confectioners' sugar, and serve at once.

MAKES **4** SERVINGS

WHITE CHOCOLATE MOUSSE

This mouth-watering mousse is a wonderful dessert for entertaining. Busy cooks will appreciate the fact that is can be kept up to 2 days before serving.

1³/₄ pounds white chocolate

5 egg yolks

¹/₂ cup plus 1 tablespoon
confectioners' sugar (2 ounces)

3 cups heavy cream

¹/₄ cup Grand Marnier *or* other
liqueur

PREPARATION AND SERVING Melt white chocolate slowly in a double boiler over very low heat or melt in a microwave oven on medium or medium-low power, stirring occasionally. Cool to 95°F. Combine egg yolks and confectioners' sugar in a bowl. Whip until pale yellow and ribbon forms when trailed from whisk. In another bowl, whip cream to soft peaks and then add liqueur, whipping to incorporate. Fold ¹/₃ of the whipped cream into egg mixture. Thoroughly fold in melted white chocolate. Fold in remaining whipped cream and chill, covered.

MAKES ABOUT 5 CUPS

MARBLEIZED
PAN SOUFFLE

 crucial part in making a soufflé is the point to which the whites are beaten. Most soufflés that fall do so because the whites are overbeaten or overfolded.

3 ounces semisweet chocolate

2 tablespoons butter

2 tablespoons flour

Pinch salt

³/₄ cup milk

5 tablespoons sugar

3 egg yolks

2 teaspoons vanilla

2 tablespoons dark rum

**1 teaspoon instant espresso,
   dissolved in 1 tablespoon boiling
   water**

4 egg whites

1¹/₂ cup heavy cream, whipped

PREPARATION Heat oven to 425°F. Generously butter and dust with sugar a 9-inch pie pan or gratin dish that you can use as a serving dish. In a small saucepan over hot water, melt chocolate. Stir until smooth and remove from heat. Melt butter in a heavy saucepan. Stir flour and cook, stirring, about 2 minutes, being careful not to allow to color. Add salt and slowly whisk in milk, cooking until smooth and bubbly, about 3 minutes. Stir in 2 tablespoons sugar. In a small bowl, lightly beat egg yolks. Stir about ¹/₄ of the hot milk mixture into yolks and add yolk mixture to pan, stirring over lowest heat for about 1 minute. Remove from heat. Stir in vanilla and rum.

Blend ¹/₃ cup of the custard and espresso into melted chocolate. In a mixing bowl, beat egg whites to soft peaks. Gradually add remaining 3 tablespoons sugar and continue beating until whites just form firm peaks, being careful not to overbeat. Stir a large spoonful of whites into both chocolate and rum custards to lighten. Gently fold ¹/₂ of remaining whites into each of the custards. Spoon alternating dollops of chocolate custard and rum custard into prepared pan. Using a spatula, quickly and gently marbleize mixtures.

COOKING AND SERVING Bake in center of preheated oven until puffed but still wobbly in center, about 10 minutes. Serve at once with whipped cream.

MAKES ❹ SERVINGS

I n the Americanized version of this quick but elegant dessert, dry white wine is used instead of Marsala, and pure maple syrup, rather than sugar, provides the sweetness.

4 egg yolks

1/3 cup pure maple syrup

6 tablespoons dry white wine

1/4 cup broken walnut meats,
   toasted and chopped

PREPARATION Spread walnuts on a baking sheet and toast in a preheated 375°F oven 6 to 8 minutes.

COOKING AND SERVING In the top of a double boiler, whisk together egg yolks, maple syrup, and wine. Set over simmering water and cook, whisking constantly, until thickened, frothy, and quadrupled in volume, 5 to 7 minutes. Pour zabaglione into 4 dessert glasses and sprinkle with nuts. Serve immediately.

MAKES **4** SERVINGS

DRINKS

Brandied
Iced Tea
236

White Sangria with
Strawberries
237

Tropical
Passion
238

Juiced Watermelon
with Vodka
239

Iced Coffee
Frangelica
240

Pernod
Spritzer
241

Pimm's Cup
242

Bellini
Cocktail
243

Tequila Lime and
Lemonade
244

Rum and White
Grape Juice
245

Planter's Punch
246

You'll find this drink tastes quite mild and surprisingly like its namesake — but it is stronger than you think. For a bourbon variation just substitute bourbon for brandy in this recipe.

4 cups tea

10 mint sprigs

Sugar to taste

8 ounces brandy

PREPARATION Make the tea, steeping 4 mint sprigs along with the tea leaves. Remove tea and mint, add sugar to taste, and chill well. Fill glasses with ice and rub rims with fresh mint. Stir brandy into tea and pour into glasses. Garnish each glass with a sprig of mint.

MAKES 4 DRINKS

WHITE SANGRIA WITH STRAWBERRIES

~~~

Serve this strawberry-laden variation of the traditional red wine sangria during the cocktail hour as well as with dinner. It is a perfect complement for Spanish and Mexican food.

1 pint strawberries
1 orange
1½ quarts white wine
3 ounces orange liqueur
2 tablespoons sugar *or* to taste

PREPARATION Reserve 4 whole strawberries for garnish. Hull and slice the remaining strawberries. Halve the orange. Squeeze juice from half the orange; slice the other half into thin half-rounds. Combine the wine, sliced strawberries, orange juice, orange slices, and liqueur. Add sugar to taste and chill for about 1 hour. Pour white sangria into glasses and garnish each glass with a whole strawberry.

MAKES **4** DRINKS

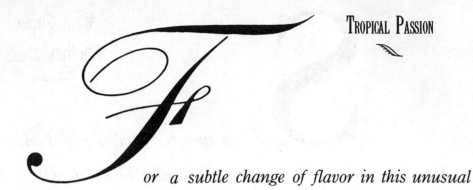

*F*or a subtle change of flavor in this unusual combination, you can substitute a ripe papaya in place of the mango.

1 ripe mango

8 ounces Alizé or other passion-
   fruit liqueur

½ cup heavy cream

8 ounces club soda

Sugar to taste

PREPARATION Cut 4 thin wedges from the mango for garnish. Peel and pit the mango and puree the flesh in a blender or food processor until smooth. Add the liqueur, heavy cream, soda, sugar, and about 3 cups of crushed ice and process briefly to combine. Pour into glasses and garnish each glass with a slice of mango.

MAKES 4 DRINKS

JUICED WATERMELON WITH VODKA

℞

If you would like to vary the taste and color of this refreshing drink, try using cantaloupe or honeydew melon in place of the watermelon or light rum in place of the vodka.

2¹⁄₂ pounds watermelon
8 ounces vodka

PREPARATION Cut 4 small wedges of watermelon for garnish. Remove the rind from the remaining watermelon. Seed watermelon, cut into chunks, and puree with the vodka in a blender or food processor until smooth. Strain through a sieve and discard any remaining seeds. Chill in freezer until slushy and almost frozen, about 1 hour. Pour into glasses and garnish with a slice of watermelon.

MAKES ❹ DRINKS

F

or an Amaretto version of this drink, sub-
stitute Amaretto for the Frangelica and almonds for the hazelnuts.

¼ cup hazelnuts (optional)

4 cups coffee

Light cream to taste

Sugar to taste and for rimming
    glasses

8 ounces Frangelica *or* other
    hazelnut liqueur

PREPARATION Heat oven to 350°F. Toast nuts in preheated oven, until fragrant and lightly browned, about 15 minutes. Cool, rub off loose skins, and mince nuts. Make 1 quart of coffee and add light cream and sugar to taste. Chill. Dip rim of each glass in water and then into sugar. Fill each glass with ice. Stir Frangelica into coffee and pour into glasses. Sprinkle with minced hazelnuts.

MAKES **4** DRINKS

With its bitter, licorice flavor and herbal aroma, Pernod teams perfectly with club soda in this simple preparation.

8 ounces Pernod
1 quart club soda

PREPARATION Fill glasses with ice. Pour Pernod into glasses, fill with soda, and stir.

MAKES 4 DRINKS

P

imm's Cup #1 is a flavorful blend of spices, herbs, and spirits. Created in London in 1841, it has since been enjoyed all over the world.

2 oranges
2 limes
1 cucumber
8 ounces Pimm's Cup #1
1 pint club soda
2 teaspoons sugar

PREPARATION Cut 4 thin slices each of orange and lime. Squeeze $1/3$ cup orange juice and 2 tablespoons lime juice. Cut 4 wedges from cucumber for garnish. Fill glasses with ice and citrus slices. Combine citrus juice, Pimm's Cup #1, club soda, and sugar and pour into glasses. Garnish each glass with a cucumber wedge.

MAKES 4 DRINKS

BELLINI COCKTAIL

*T*his light combination of peaches and champagne originated in Venice. But its popularity is sweeping America, where it has become one of the trendiest drinks.

4 large peaches
1 tablespoon sugar
½ tablespoon lemon juice
12 ounces chilled champagne

PREPARATION Peel, pit, and cut up the peaches and then puree in a blender or food processor until smooth. Moisten a double layer of cheesecloth and line a sieve with it. Press the peach puree through the cheesecloth-lined sieve, then put the puree, a bit at a time, into a sieve lined with a coffee filter and set over a bowl. Stir gently, being careful not to break the filter, until all juice has been extracted. Replace filter as needed. Chill peach juice. (Recipe can be completed to this point several hours ahead.)

SERVING Combine the sugar and the lemon juice and stir until the sugar is dissolved. Add to the peach juice. Pour 1 jigger (1½ ounces) of the peach mixture into each champagne glass. Top with about 3 ounces of chilled champagne per serving.

MAKES **4** SERVINGS

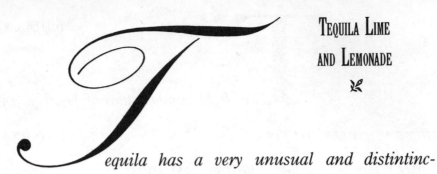

TEQUILA LIME AND LEMONADE

*T*equila has a very unusual and distintinctive taste which is herbaceous and grassy in nature. It has a natural affinity to salt and lemon or lime juice.

4 lemons
8 limes
1/2 cup sugar
3 cups water
8 ounces tequila

PREPARATION Cut 4 spirals each of lemon and lime zest for garnish. Squeeze 1/2 cup juice from lemons; 3/4 cup juice from limes. Combine the sugar and lemon and lime juices and stir until sugar is dissolved. Stir in the water and tequila. Put ice and citrus spirals in glasses. Pour in tequila, and the lime and lemonade.

VARIATION Substitute vodka for the tequila.

MAKES **4** DRINKS

This grape-garnished fruity cooler can be described as light, both in color and in taste.

1 quart chilled white grape juice
8 ounces rum
Grapes for garnish (optional)

PREPARATION Fill glasses with ice. Combine grape juice and rum and pour into glasses. Garnish each glass with a small cluster of grapes.

MAKES **4** DRINKS

P

lanter's punch is a combination of sour-
sweet-strong-and-weak, in a ratio that is the subject of debate among
the lovers of this drink.

2 large lemons

6 oranges

8 ounces dark rum

1 tablespoon grenadine

PREPARATION Cut 4 slices of lemon and 4 of orange for garnish. Squeeze $1/4$ cup lemon juice and 2 cups orange juice. Combine the juices, rum, and grenadine and pour into ice-filled glasses. Garnish each glass with lemon and orange slices.

MAKES ④ DRINKS

CREDITS

APPETIZERS AND LIGHT MEALS

APPETIZER TOASTS WITH
TWO TOPPINGS
  Deborah Madison
TOMATO AND PARMESAN
CHEESE TOPPING
  Deborah Madison
HERBED OLIVE TOPPING
  Deborah Madison
CALIFORNIA CROSTINI
  Marlena Spieler
CROSTINI WITH GRILLED
SUMMER VEGETABLES
AND SMOKED MOZZARELLA
  Brooke Dojny and
  Melanie Barnard
FENNEL WITH OLIVE OIL
  Julia della Croce
BACON AND TOMATO PITA
PIZZAS
  Brooke Dojny and
  Melanie Barnard
WALNUT GOUGERE
  Nicholas Malgieri
PATE A CHOUX
  Nicholas Malgieri
CHERRY TOMATOES FILLED
WITH GOAT CHEESE AND
THYME
  Martha Stewart
WATERCRESS CUCUMBER
SANDWICHES
  Angela Hynes
ASPARAGUS AND HAM OME-
LETS WITH BLUE CHEESE
  Brooke Dojny and
  Melanie Barnard
BASIC OMELET
  Beverly Cox
SOUR CREAM, SMOKED SALM-
ON, AND BLACK CAVIAR
OMELET
  Beverly Cox
APPLE OMELET
  Beverly Cox
ORANGE AND YOGURT
WAFFLES
  Barbara Karoff
ONION AND FENNEL
FRITTATA
  Martha Stewart

SAVORY SWISS CHARD
FRITATTA
  Brooke Dojny and
  Melanie Barnard
LA PIPERADE
  Elene Margot Kolb
BUTTERMILK CORNMEAL
PANCAKES
  Jane and Michael Stern

SOUPS

COLD NECTARINE SOUP
  Elizabeth Riely
BRUSSELS SPROUTS AND
BEER-CHEESE SOUP
  Melanie Barnard
SPRING VEGETABLE SOUP
  Anne Willan
RED SNAPPER SOUP
  Kenneth Pulomena
RED SNAPPER STEW
  Jonathan Waxman
THE TRELLIS CHEESE SOUP
  Marcel Desalniers
TOMATO AND GARLIC SOUP
  Cathy Gunst
CHILLED SUGAR SNAP PEA
SOUP WITH MINT
  Sid Larson and Greg Wescott
COUNTRY CORN CHOWDER
  David and Ellen Gibson
FENNEL SOUP WITH CHEESE
  Pam Perseghian
PEPPERY LENTIL SOUP
  Pam Perseghian
CORNED BEEF AND CABBAGE
SOUP
  Pam Perseghian
CHILLED AVOCADO SOUP
WITH CORIANDER SALSA
  Melanie Barnard
CHICKEN SOUP WITH
ALMONDS
  Melanie Barnard
SAUSAGE AND SUCCOTASH
SOUP
  Melanie Barnard
SUMMER GARDEN
MINESTRONE
  Melanie Barnard

ORANGE AND CARROT SOUP
  Barbara Karoff
SMOKY SWEET-POTATO SOUP
WITH SOUR CREAM AND
JALAPENOS
  Alice Waters and Therese Shere

PASTAS, GRAINS AND BREADS

RAVIOLI WITH FRESH TOMA-
TO AND GARLIC SAUCE
  Melanie Barnard
WINTER VEGETABLE PASTA
  Barry Wine
BOW TIES WITH SPICY CHICK-
EN AND SWEET PEPPERS
  Tracy Pikhart Ritter
VERMICELLI WITH ZUCCHINI
AND SALMON
  Brooke Dojny and
  Melanie Barnard
LINGUINE WITH TURKEY AND
MUSHROOMS
  Betsy Schultz
HAM AND ORZO SALAD WITH
MUSTARD THYME
VINAIGRETTE
  Brooke Dojny and
  Melanie Barnard
RIGATONI WITH BACON,
TOMATO, AND RICOTTA
  Betsy Schultz
BOW TIES WITH ARUGULA,
BACON, AND PARMESAN
CHEESE
  Brooke Dojny and
  Melanie Barnard
FUSILLI WITH VEAL AND
ARTICHOKES
  Betsy Schultz
RISOTTO WITH HAM AND
ASPARAGUS
  Melanie Barnard
RISOTTO WITH ARTICHOKES
  Pat Opler
QUICK PAELLA
  Melanie Barnard
WEHANI RICE WITH PORT AND
PECANS
  Michelle Urvater

MEXICAN FRIED RICE
   Michelle Urvater
SAFFRON RICE WITH SUN-
DRIED TOMATOES
   Bruce Molzan
SCALLOP AND BACON
JAMBALAYA
   Pam Parseghian
ORIENTAL PILAF WITH
PEACHES
   Elizabeth Riely
LEMON AND ALMOND PILAF
   Michelle Urvater
VEGETABLE ORIENTAL
NOODLES
   Karen McCoy-Tack
POPOVERS
   Judith Sutton
BLUEBERRY CORN MUFFINS
   Anne Byrn
BLUE AND YELLOW CORN-
STICKS AND MUFFINS
   Anne Lyndsay Greer
CORN MUFFINS WITH SPICED
HAM
   Amy Cotler and
   Sherry Baltramini-Pincus
SAFFRON CORNBREAD
   Sandra Gluck
HERBED POTATO BISCUITS
   Judith Jamison
HERB CHEESE BISCUITS
   Anne Byrn

SEAFOOD

BROILED OYSTERS WITH
SHALLOT WINE SAUCE
   Anne Byrne
SAUSAGE AND OYSTERS
   Miriam Ungerer
OYSTERS IN CHAMPAGNE
SAUCE
   Barbara Kafka
BAKED OYSTERS WITH CHILI-
CORIANDER PESTO
   Mark Ellman
MUSSELS AND TOMATO
PERNOD BUTTER
   Greg Zifchak

SCALLOPS IN WHITE WINE,
SHALLOTS, AND HERBS
   Wayne Ludvigen
CAJUN SHRIMP SANDWICH
   Melanie Barnard
SHRIMP WITH TUNA
FISH SAUCE
   Anna Teresa Callen
SHRIMP ROCKEFELLER
   Palm-Aire, Pomano Beach,
Florida
GRILLED SHRIMP WITH
CILANTRO
   Michael McCarty
SKEWERED SHRIMP AND
SCALLIONS
   Miriam Ungerer
TUNA STEAKS STUFFED WITH
SAGE AND SMOKED GOUDA
   Melanie Barnard
GROUPER EN ESCABECHE
   Ralph Pausina
ISLAND ESCABECHE
   Laurence Sombke
GRILLED SALMON WITH CHI-
NESE MUSTARDS AND LEEKS
   Barry Wine
SALMON IN COURT BOUILLON
WITH HERB BUTTER
   Paul Bertolli
SIZZLED SALMON WITH LIME
BUTTER
   Melanie Barnard
HALIBUT WITH SMOKED SALM-
ON AND DILL BUTTER
   Michael McLaughlin
POACHED HALIBUT WITH CAR-
ROTS AND CREAM SAUCE
   Pam Parseghian
RED SNAPPER WITH SWEET
AND HOT PEPPERS
   Michael McLaughlin
FISH STEAKS WITH THYME
   Miriam Ungerer
SWORDFISH WITH TOMATOES
AND BASIL
   Michael McLaughlin
GRILLED SWORDFISH WITH TO-
MATO-BASIL BEURRE BLANC
   Michael McCarty

GRILLED SWORDFISH
SANDWICH
   Brendan Walsh
TUNA STEAKS WITH CAPER
MAYONNAISE
   Melanie Barnard
GRILLED TUNA WITH BASIL
AND RED PEPPERS
   Bill King

MEATS

BEEF TENDERLOIN WITH
SAGE, ROSEMARY, AND
ARUGULA
   Evan Kleiman
STEAK WITH MUSHROOMS
AND RED WINE SAUCE
   Elizabeth Riely
GRILLED STEAK TOPPED
WITH PEPPER AND GARLIC
BUTTER
   Ken Schloss
STEAKS WITH BOURBON-
GLAZED ONIONS
   Melanie Barnard
VEAL CHOPS SAUTE
   Sheryl Julian
FOUR ONION RELISH
   Sheryl Julian
VEAL SCALLOPS IN LIME
CREAM SAUCE
   Melanie Barnard
BROILED LAMB CHOPS ON A
BED OF WATERCRESS
   Melanie Barnard
GRILLED LAMB WITH MINT
SAUCE AND CUCUMBER
RAITA
   Melanie Barnard
PORK CUTLETS WITH TOMA-
TO CITRUS SAUCE
   Melanie Barnard
STIR-FRIED PORK WITH
BROCCOLI
   Brooke Dojny and
   Melanie Barnard
MIDWEST PORK TENDERLOIN
SANDWICH
   Jane and Michael Stern

SWEET SAUSAGE WITH
GRAPES
  Anne Byrn
CALF'S LIVER WITH PARSLEY
AND LEMON
  Melanie Barnard

POULTRY

PERFECT FRIED CHICKEN
  Miriam Ungerer
ROSEMARY FRIED CHICKEN
  Pam Parseghian
CHILI SPICED FRIED CHICKEN
  Faye Levy
FRIED CHICKEN SALAD WITH
SWEET ONIONS
  Ann Byrn
GRILLED CHICKEN ON
ARUGULA SALAD
  Pam Parseghian
CHICKEN SALAD WITH THYME
AND RED ONION VINAIGRETTE
  Pam Parseghian
CHICKEN WITH SMOKED MOZ-
ZARELLA AND PESTO
  Amy Cotler and
  Sherry Beltramini-Pincus
GRILLED CHICKEN BREASTS
WITH CILANTRO-LIME
BUTTER
  Faye Levy
CHICKEN WITH MUSHROOMS
AND GARLIC
  Barbara Kafka
SAUTEED CHICKEN WITH TAR-
RAGON AND MUSHROOMS
  Pam Parseghian
CHICKEN BREASTS WITH SUM-
MER SQUASH AND YELLOW
PEPPERS
  Sheryl Julian
STEAMED BREAST OF
CHICKEN WITH RED-ONION
MARMALADE
  Lion's Rock Restaurant, New
York
CHICKEN STUFFED WITH
BLUE CHEESE AND WALNUTS
  Elizabeth Riely

BROILED GINGER-ORANGE
GAME HENS
  Melanie Barnard
GRILLED GINGER DUCK
BREASTS WITH PEACHES
  Melanie Barnard

VEGETABLES

MASHED POTATOES WITH
ROASTED SHALLOT
HOLLANDAISE
  Barry Wine
LEEKS WITH VINEGAR SAUCE
  Melanie Barnard
EGGPLANT, ZUCCHINI, AND
BELL PEPPER SAUTE
  Ruggero Gadaldi
SUGAR-SNAP PEAS WITH
SCALLIONS
  Melanie Barnard
SIMPLE GREEN BEANS
  Judith Jamison
LEMON CARROTS
  Melanie Barnard
KALE TIMBALES WITH
SAUTEED RADISHES
  Susan Herrmann Loomis
COUNTRY-STYLE LIMA BEANS
  Larry Forgione
SAUTE OF TOMATOES
  Elizabeth Wheeler
SAUTEED MUSHROOMS WITH
GARLIC
  Brad Cole
PARSNIPS WITH ORANGE
JUICE AND HAM
  Michael McLaughlin
PARSLEY FRITTERS
  Carol Cutler
ASPARAGUS WITH COUNTRY
HAM AND LEMON BUTTER
  Larry Forgione
ASPARAGUS BUNDLES WITH
CORNICHON VINAIGRETTE
  Martha Stewart
SAUTEED BROCCOLI RABE
WITH GARLIC
  Julia dellaCroce
SPICY STIR-FRIED EGGPLANT
  Nina Simond

CARROTS, PEPPERS, AND CAB-
BAGE IN LETTUCE
  Martha Stewart
BROWNED BRUSSELS
SPROUTS
  Larry Forgione
SAUTEED ZUCCHINI WITH
WALNUTS
  Marlene Sorosky
VEGETABLE MEDLEY
  Barbara Kafka
GREEN-PEA AND MINT SAUCE
  Barbara Kafka
VEGETABLES AND EGGS
  Barbara Kafka

SALADS AND DRESSINGS

BREAD SALAD WITH ONIONS
  Alice Waters and Therese Shere
SPINACH SALAD WITH TOMA-
TO-SHALLOT DRESSING
  The Verandah Club,
Dallas, Texas
CREAMY COLESLAW
  Anne Lindsay Greer
WALDORF SALAD
  Melanie Barnard
ARUGULA SALAD
  Susan Herrmann Loomis
CUCUMBER AND PEPPER
SALAD
  Pam Parseghian
CURRIED CHICKEN SALAD
WITH FRESH BASIL
  Melanie Barnard
MESCLUN SALAD
  Alice Waters and Therese Shere
SALAMI AND CHEESE SALAD
  Michael Mc Laughlin
TOMATO AND MOZZARELLA
SALAD
  Pam Parseghian
SUMMER MELON SALAD
  Alice Waters and Patricia Curtan
MEDLEY SALAD WITH
VINAIGRETTE
  Pam Parseghian
HERB VINAIGRETTE
  Pam Parseghian

BULGUR GARDEN SALAD
  Michael McLaughlin
SEAFOOD AND BARLEY SALAD
  Michael McLaughlin
PROVENCAL BEAN SALAD
  Kathy Gunst
RADISH AND FENNEL SALAD
  Alice Waters and Therese Shere
SALAD OF DARK GREENS,
RADICCHIO, AND SHRIMP
  Roberta Frechette
WARM FINNISH POTATO
SALAD
  Pam Parseghian
CUCUMBER AND BRIE SALAD
  Pam Parseghian

COOKIES AND CAKES

PEANUT BUTTER COOKIES
  Miriam Ungerer
CLASSIC SHORTBREAD
  Helen Witty
GINGER SHORTBREAD
  Helen Witty
ORANGE HAZELNUT
BROWNIES
  Barbara Souse
DEVIL'S FOOD CAKE
  Miriam Ungerer
CREAMY CHOCOLATE
FROSTING
  Miriam Ungerer
BUTTERSCOTCH PUDDING
CAKE
  Regina Schrambling
BRANDIED ESPRESSO
PUDDING CAKE
  Regina Schrambling
RUM PUDDING CAKE
  Regina Schrambling
WALNUT FUDGE PUDDING
CAKE
  Regina Schrambling

DESSERTS

PEACHES AND WHITE WINE
ICE
  Elizabeth Riley

PEACHES IN HOT-BUTTERED
RUM
  Elizabeth Riely
PEACH CREPES
  Gurney's Inn, Montauk, New
York
NECTARINES POACHED IN
PORT
  Elizabeth Riely
NECTARINES AND PLUMS
WITH PARMESAN
  Brooke Dojny
APRICOTS WITH AMARETTI
  Brooke Dojny
PEARS WITH MASCARPONE
  Anna Teresa Callen
PEARS STUFFED WITH
GORGONZOLA
  Brooke Dojny
POACHED PEARS WITH
KIRSCH SABAYON
  Jimmy Schmitt
BAKED PEARS WITH SHRED-
DED CHOCOLATE
  Brooke Dojny
ICY ORANGES WITH CINAM-
MON AND CLOVES
  Judith Jamison
BLOOD ORANGES WITH
NUTMEG
  Brooke Dojny
ALMOND- AND CHEESE-
STUFFED FIGS
  Anna Teresa Callen
FIGS WITH MASCARPONE
  Brooke Dojny
TROPICAL FRUIT SALAD WITH
PECANS AND CAMPARI
  Anna Teresa Callen
GRILLED FRESH PINEAPPLE
  Miriam Ungerer
RIESLING-MARINATED
STRAWBERRIES
  Brooke Dojny
MINTED STRAWBERRIES AND
SOUR CREAM
  Melanie Barnard
MIXED FRUIT PLATTER
  Martha Stewart

MELON IN PORT WITH
CORIANDER CREAM
  Brooke Dojny
CLOVE-STUDDED APPLES
  Brooke Dojny
FRITTERS WITH CINNAMON
WINE SAUCE
  Copeland Marks
BANANA FRITTERS
  Thayer Wine
WHITE CHOCOLATE MOUSSE
  Albert Kumin
MARBLEIZED PAN SOUFFLE
  Melanie Barnard
MAPLE-WALNUT
ZABAGLIONE
  Melanie Barnard

DRINKS

BRANDIED ICED TEA
  Pam Parseghian
WHITE SANGRIA WITH
STRAWBERRIES
  Pam Parseghian
TROPICAL PASSION
  Pam Parseghian
JUICED WATERMELON WITH
VODKA
  Pam Parseghian
ICED COFFEE FRANGELICA
  Pam Parseghian
PERNOD SPRITZER
  Pam Parseghian
PIMM'S CUP
  Pam Parseghian
BELLINI COCKTAIL
  Elizabeth Riely
TEQUILA LIME AND
LEMONADE
  Pam Parseghian
RUM AND WHITE GRAPE JUICE
  Pam Parseghian
PLANTER'S PUNCH
  Pam Parseghian

INDEX

ALMOND(S)
Almond- and Cheese-Stuffed Figs, 220
Chicken Soup with Almonds, 48
Lemon and Almond Pilaf, 73

APPETIZERS, 10

APPLE(S)
Apple Filling, 25
Apple Omelet, 24
Clove-Studded Apples, 228
Waldorf Salad, 177

APRICOT(S)
Apricots with Amaretti, 213

ARTICHOKE(S)
Fusilli with Veal and Artichokes, 64
Risotto with Artichokes, 66

ARUGULA
Arugula Salad, 178
Beef Tenderloin with Sage, Rosemary, and Arugula, 114
Grilled Chicken on Arugula Salad, 178
Medley Salad with Vinaigrette, 185
Warm Finnish Potato Salad, 192

ASPARAGUS,
Asparagus and Ham Omelets with Blue Cheese, 121
Asparagus Bundles with Cornichon Vinaigrette, 163
Asparagus with Country Ham and Lemon Butter, 162
Risotto with Ham and Asparagus, 65

AVOCADO
Chilled Avocado Soup with Coriander Salsa, 47

BACON
Arugula Salad, 178
Bacon and Tomato Pita Pizzas, 16
Rigatoni with Bacon, Tomato, and Ricotta, 62
Scallop and Bacon Jambalaya, 71

BANANA(S)
Banana Fritters, 230

BARBECUE and GRILLED
Grilled Chicken Breasts with Cilantro-Lime Butter, 137
Grilled Chicken on Arugula Salad, 134
Grilled Fresh Pineapple, 223
Grilled Ginger Duck Breasts with Peaches, 144
Grilled Lamb with Mint Sauce and Cucumber Raita, 122
Grilled Salmon with Chinese Mustard and Leeks, 98
Grilled Shrimp with Cilantro, 93
Grilled Steak Topped with Pepper and Garlic Butter, 116
Grilled Swordfish Sandwich, 109
Grilled Swordfish with Beurre Blanc, 107
Grilled Tuna with Basil and Red Peppers, 111
Skewered Shrimp and Scallions, 94
Swordfish with Tomatoes and Basil, 106
Tuna Steaks Stuffed with Sage and Smoked Gouda, 95

BASIL
Curried Chicken Salad with Fresh Basil, 180
Grilled Tuna with Basil and Red Peppers, 111
Sauté of Tomatoes, 158
Swordfish with Tomatoes and Basil, 106

BEAN(S)
Country-Style Lima Beans, 157
Provençal Bean Salad, 189
Sausage and Succotash Soup, 49
Simple Green Beans, 153

BEEF
Beef Tenderloin with Sage, Rosemary, and Arugula, 114
Grilled Steak Topped with Pepper and Garlic Butter, 116
Steaks with Bourbon-Glazed Onions, 117
Steak with Mushrooms and Red-Wine Sauce, 115

BEVERAGES, 236

BIBB LETTUCE
Carrots, Peppers, and Cabbage in Lettuce Cups, 166
Fried Chicken Salad with Sweet Onions, 133
Waldorf Salad, 177

BISCUIT(S) and ROLL(S)
Herb Cheese Biscuits, 81
Herbed Potato Biscuits, 80

BLUE CHEESE
Asparagus and Ham Omelets with Blue Cheese, 21
Chicken Stuffed with Blue Cheese and Walnuts, 142

BLUEBERRIES
Blueberry Corn Muffins, 76

BOSTON LETTUCE
Fried Chicken Salad with Sweet Onions, 133
Waldorf Salad, 177

BRANDY
Brandied Espresso Pudding Cake, 203
Brandied Iced Tea, 236

BREAD(S), *see also* **MUFFIN(S)**
Cheddar Cheese Popovers, 75
Parmesan-Basil Popovers, 75
Popovers, 75
Saffron Cornbread, 79

BRIE
Cucumber and Brie Salad, 93

BROCCOLI
Stir-Fried Pork with Broccoli, 124
Vegetable Medley with Green-Pea and Mint Sauce, 169

BROCCOLI RABE
Sautéed Broccoli Rabe with Garlic, 164

BROWNIES
Orange Hazelnut Brownies, 199

BRUSSELS SPROUT(S)
Browned Brussels Sprouts, 167
Brussels Sprouts and Beer-Cheese Soup, 35
Vegetable Medley with Green-Pea and Mint Sauce, 169

BUTTER(S)
Cilantro-lime butter, 137
Dill butter, 102
Herb butter, 99
Pepper and garlic butter, 116
Tomato and Pernod butter, 88

CABBAGE
Carrots, Peppers, and Cabbage in Lettuce Cups, 166
Corned Beef and Cabbage Soup, 46
Creamy Coleslaw, 176

CAKE(S)
Brandied Espresso Pudding Cake, 203
Butterscotch Pudding Cake, 202
Devil's Food Cake, 200
Rum Pudding Cake, 204
Walnut Fudge Pudding Cake, 205

CARROTS
Carrots, Peppers, and Cabbage in Lettuce Cups, 166
Lemon Carrots, 154
Orange and Carrot Soup, 61
Poached Halibut with Carrots and Cream Sauce, 103
Vegetable Medley with Green-Pea and Mint Sauce, 169
Vegetable Oriental Noodles, 74

CAVIAR
Sour Cream, Smoked Salmon, and Black Caviar Omelet, 23

CHAMPAGNE
Oysters in Champagne Sauce, 86

CHEDDAR
Brussels Sprouts and Beer-Cheese Soup, 35
Salami and Cheese Salad, 182
The Trellis Cheese Soup, 39

CHEESE(S), see also names of cheeses
Almond- and Cheese-Stuffed Figs, 220
Fennel Soup with Cheese, 44
Figs with Mascarpone, 221
Herb Cheese Biscuits, 81
Nectarines and Plums with Parmesan, 212
Pears Stuffed with Gorgonzola, 215
Pears with Mascarpone, 214
Salami and Cheese Salad, 182
The Trellis Cheese Soup, 39

CHICKEN
Bow Ties with Spicy Chicken and Sweet Peppers, 58
Chicken Salad with Thyme and Red Onion Vinaigrette, 135
Chicken Soup with Almonds, 48
Chicken Stuffed with Blue Cheese and Walnuts, 142
Chicken with Mushrooms & Garlic, 138
Chicken with Smoked Mozzarella and Pesto, 136
Chili-Spiced Fried Chicken, 132
Curried Chicken Salad with Basil, 180
Fried Chicken Salad with Sweet Onions, 133
Grilled Chicken Breasts with Cilantro-Lime Butter, 137
Grilled Chicken on Arugula Salad, 134
Perfect Fried Chicken, 130
Rosemary Fried Chicken, 131
Sautéed Chicken with Tarragon and Mushrooms, 139
Steamed Breasts of Chicken with Red-Onion Marmalade, 141

CHILI
Chili-Spiced Fried Chicken, 132

CHOCOLATE
Baked Pears with Shredded Chocolate, 217
Creamy Chocolate Frosting, 201
Devil's Food Cake, 200
Marbleized Pan Soufflé, 232
Walnut Fudge Pudding Cake, 205
White Chocolate Mousse, 231

CHOWDERS
Country Corn Chowder, 43

CILANTRO
Grilled Chicken Breasts with Cilantro-Lime Butter, 137
Grilled Shrimp with Cilantro, 93

CLAM(S)
Quick Paella, 67

COLESLAW
Creamy Coleslaw, 176

COOKIES and BARS
Classic Shortbread, 197
Ginger Shortbread, 197
Peanut Butter Cookies, 196

CORN
Country Corn Chowder, 43
Sausage and Succotash Soup, 49

CORNISH GAME HENS
Broiled Ginger-Orange Game Hens, 143

CORNMEAL
Blue and Yellow Cornsticks and Muffins, 77
Blueberry Corn Muffins, 76
Buttermilk Cornmeal Pancakes, 30
Corn Muffins with Spiced Ham, 78
Saffron Cornbread, 79

CREPES
Peach Crepes, 210

CROSTINI
California Crostini, 13
Crostini with Grilled Summer
Vegetables

CUCUMBER(S)
Cucumber and Brie Salad, 193
Cucumber and Pepper Salad, 179
Cucumber Raita, 122
Watercress Cucumber Sandwich,
20

CURRY(IED)
Curried Chicken Salad with Basil,
180

DESSERTS, *see specific types*

DILL(ED)
Halibut with Smoked Salmon and
Dill Butter, 102

DRESSING(S)
Balsamic and Mustard-Seed
Dressing, 182
Balsamic Vinaigrette, 192
Black-Olive Vinaigrette, 189
Cornichon Vinaigrette, 163
Herb and Jalapeño Vinaigrette, 187
Herb Vinaigrette, 186
Lemon and Basil Vinaigrette, 188
Mustard-Thyme Vinaigrette, 61
Pimiento Dressing, 134
Tomato-Shallot Dressing, 175

DUCK
Grilled Ginger Duck Breasts with
Peaches, 144

EGG(S)
Apple Omelet, 24
Asparagus and Ham Omelets with
Blue Cheese, 21
Basic Omelet, 22
La Piperade, 29
Onion and Fennel Frittata, 27
Savory Swiss Chard Frittata, 28
Sour Cream, Smoked Salmon, and
Black Caviar Omelet, 23
Vegetables with Eggs, 171

EGGPLANT
Eggplant, Zucchini, and Bell-
Pepper Sauté, 151
Spicy Stir-Fried Eggplant, 165

ESCAROLE
Salad of Dark Greens, Radicchio,
and Shrimp, 191
Spinach Salad, 175

FENNEL
Fennel Soup with Cheese, 44
Fennel with Olive Oil, 15
Onion and Fennel Frittata, 27
Radish and Fennel Salad, 190
Winter Vegetable Pasta, 57

FIG(S)
Almond- and Cheese-Stuffed Figs,
220
Figs with Mascarpone, 221

FISH, *see also specific types*
Fish Steaks with Thyme, 105
Grouper en Escabeche, 96
Halibut with Smoked Salmon and
Dill Butter, 102
Island Escabeche, 97
Poached Halibut with Carrots and
Cream Sauce, 103
Red Snapper with Sweet and Hot
Peppers, 104
Swordfish with Tomatoes and
Basil, 106

FLOUNDER
Island Escabeche, 97

FRITTERS
Banana Fritters, 161
Fritters with Cinnamon Wine
Sauce, 229
Parsley Fritters, 161

FRUIT, *see also specific page*
Grilled Fresh Pineapple, 223
Melon in Port with Coriander
Cream, 227
Mixed Fruit Platter, 226
Summer Melon Salad, 184

Tropical Fruit Salad with Pecans
and Campari, 222

FROSTING(S) and ICING(S)
Creamy Chocolate Frosting, 201
Grand Marnier Ganache Icing, 199

GARLIC
Chicken with Mushrooms and
Garlic, 138
Ravioli with Fresh Tomato and
Garlic Sauce, 56
Red-Pepper and Garlic Sauce, 41
Sautéed Broccoli Rabe with Garlic,
164
Sautéed Mushrooms with Garlic,
159
Tomato and Garlic Soup, 40

GINGER
Broiled Ginger-Orange Game
Hens, 143
Ginger Shortbread, 198
Grilled Ginger Duck Breasts with
Peaches, 144

GOAT CHEESE
Cherry Tomatoes Filled with Goat
Cheese, 19

GOUDA
Tuna Steaks Stuffed with Sage and
Smoked Gouda, 95
Gougere, 17

GRAIN(S)
Bulgur Garden Salad, 187
Lemon and Almond Pilaf, 73
Mexican Fried Rice, 69
Oriental Pilaf with Peaches, 72
Risotto with Artichokes, 66
Risotto with Ham and Asparagus,
65
Saffron Rice with Sun-Dried
Tomatoes, 70
Scallop and Bacon Jambalaya, 71
Seafood and Barley Salad, 188
Quick Paella, 67
Wehani Rice with Port and
Pecans, 68

GREEN BEAN(S), *see* **BEAN(S)**

GRUYERE
Fennel Soup with Cheese, 44
Salami and Cheese Salad, 182

HALIBUT
Halibut with Smoked Salmon and
Dill Butter, 102
Poached Halibut with Carrots and
Cream Sauce, 103

HAM
Asparagus with Country Ham and
Lemon Butter, 162
Ham and Orzo Salad with Mustard-
Thyme Vinaigrette, 61
La Piperade, 29
Parsnips with Orange Juice and
Ham, 160
Risotto with Ham and Asparagus,
65

JALAPENO(S)
Herb and Jalapeño Vinaigrette, 187
Smoky Sweet-Potato Soup with
Sour Cream and Jalapeños, 52

KALE
Kale Timbales with Sautéed
Radishes, 155

LAMB
Broiled Lamb Chops on a Bed of
Sautéed Watercress, 121
Grilled Lamb with Mint Sauce and
Cucumber Raita, 122

LEEK(S)
Grilled Salmon with Chinese
Mustard and Leeks, 98
Leeks with Vinegar Sauce, 150
Winter Vegetable Pasta, 57

LENTIL(S)
Peppery Lentil Soup, 45

LIMA BEAN(S), *see* **BEAN(S)**

LIVER
Calf's Liver with Parsley and
Lemon, 127

MAYONNAISE
Caper Mayonnaise, 110
Walnut Oil Mayonnaise, 177

MELON(S)
Melon in Port with Coriander
Cream, 227
Summer Melon Salad, 184

MINT(ED)
Chilled Sugar-Snap Pea Soup with
Mint, 42

MOUSSE
White Chocolate Mousse, 231

MOZZARELLA
Chicken with Smoked Mozzarella
and Pesto, 136
Crostini with Grilled Summer
Vegetables and Smoked
Mozzarella, 14
Tomato and Mozzarella Salad, 183

MUFFINS
Blueberry Corn Muffins, 76
Blue and Yellow Cornsticks and
Muffins, 77
Corn Muffins with Spiced Ham, 78

MUSHROOMS
Chicken with Mushrooms and
Garlic, 138
Linguine with Turkey and
Mushrooms, 60
Sautéed Chicken with Tarragon and
Mushrooms, 139
Sautéed Mushrooms with Garlic,
159
Steak with Mushrooms and Red-
Wine Sauce, 115

MUSSEL(S)
Mussels with Tomato and Pernod
Butter, 88
Spring Vegetable Soup, 36
Quick Paella, 67

NECTARINES
Cold Nectarine Soup, 34
Nectarines and Plums with
Parmesan, 212
Nectarines Poached in Port, 211

NOODLE(S)
Vegetable Oriental Noodles, 74

OMELET(S)
Apple Omelet, 24
Asparagus and Ham Omelets with
Blue Cheese, 21
Basic Omelet, 22
Sour Cream, Smoked Salmon, and
Black Caviar Omelet, 23

ONION(S)
Bread Salad with Onions, 174
Chicken Salad with Thyme and Red
Onion Vinaigrette, 135
Four Onion relish, 119
Fried Chicken Salad with Sweet
Onions, 133
Onion and Fennel Frittata, 27
Steaks with Bourbon-Glazed
Onions, 117
Steamed Breast of Chicken with
Red-Onion Marmalade, 141

ORANGE(S)
Icy Oranges with Cinnamon and
Cloves, 218
Blood Oranges with Nutmeg, 219
Orange and Carrot Soup, 61
Orange and Yogurt Waffles, 26
Orange Hazelnut Brownies, 199

OYSTER(S)
Baked Oysters with Chile-
Coriander Pesto, 87
Broiled Oysters with Shallot Wine
Sauce, 84
Oysters in Champagne Sauce, 86
Sausages and Oysters, 85

PANCAKE(S)
Buttermilk Cornmeal Pancakes, 30

PARMESAN
Nectarines and Plums with
  Parmesan, 212

PARSLEY
Calf's Liver with Parsley and
  Lemon, 127
Parsley Fritters, 161

PARSNIPS
Parsnips with Orange Juice and
  Ham, 160

PASTAS
Bow Ties with Spicy Chicken and
  Sweet Peppers, 58
Fusilli with Veal and Artichokes, 64
Ham and Orzo Salad with Mustard
  Thyme Vinaigrette, 61
Linguine with Turkey and
  Mushrooms, 60
Ravioli with Fresh Tomato and
  Garlic Sauce, 56
Rigatoni with Bacon, Tomato, and
  Ricotta, 62
Vegetable Oriental Noodles, 74
Vermicelli with Zucchini and
  Smoked Salmon, 59
Winter Vegetable Pasta, 57

PASTRY
Pâte à Choux, 18

PEA(S)
Chilled Sugar-Snap Pea Soup with
  Mint, 42
Salad of Dark Greens, Radicchio
  and Shrimp, 191
Spring Vegetable Soup, 36
Sugar-Snap Peas with Scallions,
  152
Vegetable Medley with Green-Pea
  and Mint Sauce, 169
Peanut Butter Cookies, 196

PEACH(ES)
Grilled Ginger Duck Breasts with
  Peaches, 144
Oriental Pilaf with Peaches, 72
Peach Crepes, 210

Peaches and White-Wine Ice, 208
Peaches in Hot-Buttered Rum, 209

PEAR(S)
Baked Pears with Shredded
  Chocolate, 217
Pears Stuffed with Gorgonzola, 215
Pears with Mascarpone, 214
Poached Pears with Kirsch
  Sabayon, 216

PECANS
Wehani Rice with Port and Pecans,
  68

PEPPER(S)
Bow Ties with Spicy Chicken and
  Sweet Peppers, 58
Carrots, Peppers, and Cabbage in
  Lettuce Cups, 166
Chicken Breasts with Summer
  Squash and Yellow Pepper, 140
Cucumber and Pepper Salad, 179
Eggplant, Zucchini, and Bell-
  Pepper Sauté, 151
Grilled Tuna with Basil and Red
  Peppers, 111
La Piperade, 29
Red Pepper and Garlic Sauce, 41
Red Snapper with Sweet and Hot
  Peppers, 104
Smoky Sweet Potato Soup with
  Sour Cream and Jalapeños, 52

Pesto, 136

PILAF
Lemon and Almond Pilaf, 73
Oriental Pilaf with Peaches, 72

PIZZA(S)
Bacon and Tomato Pita Pizzas, 116

PLUM(S)
Nectarines and Plums with
  Parmesan, 212

PORK
Midwest Pork Tenderloin
  Sandwich, 125

Pork Cutlets with Tomato Citrus
  Sauce, 123
Stir-Fried Pork with Broccoli, 124

POTATOE(S)
Mashed Potatoes with Roasted
  Shallot Hollandaise, 148
Red Snapper Stew, 38
Warm Finnish Potato Salad, 192

POULTRY, 129

RADICCHIO
Salad of Dark Greens, Radicchio,
  and Shrimp, 191
Spinach Salad with Tomato-Shallot
  Dressing, 175

RADISH(ES)
Kale Timbales with Sautéed
  Radishes, 155
Radish and Fennel Salad, 190

RAVIOLI
Ravioli with Fresh Tomato and
  Garlic Sauce, 56

RED SNAPPER
Red Snapper Soup, 37
Red Snapper Stew, 38
Red Snapper with Sweet and Hot
  Peppers, 104

RED WINE
Fritters with Cinnamon Wine
  Sauce, 229
Steak with Mushrooms and Red-
  Wine Sauce, 115

RELISH
Four Onion Relish, 119

RICE, *see* **GRAINS**

RISOTTO
Risotto with Artichokes, 66
Risotto with Ham and Asparagus,
  65

ROLLS, *see* **BISCUITS**

ROMAINE
Chicken Salad with Thyme and Red
  Onion Vinaigrette, 135
Medley Salad with Vinaigrette, 185
Salad of Dark Greens, Radicchio,
  and Shrimp, 191

RUM
Marbleized Pan Soufflé, 232
Peaches in Hot-Buttered Rum, 209
Planter's Punch, 246
Rum and White Grape Juice, 245
Rum Pudding Cake, 204

SAFFRON
Saffron Cornbread, 79
Saffron Rice with Sun-Dried
  Tomatoes, 70

SALADS
Arugula Salad, 178
Bread Salad with Onions, 174
Bulgur Garden Salad, 187
Chicken Salad with Thyme and Red
  Onion Vinaigrette, 135
Cucumber and Brie Salad, 193
Cucumber and Pepper Salad, 179
Curried Chicken Salad with Basil,
  180
Fried Chicken Salad with Sweet
  Onions, 133
Grilled Chicken on Arugula Salad,
  134
Ham and Orzo Salad with Mustard-
  Thyme Vinaigrette, 61
Medley Salad with Vinaigrette, 185
Mesclun Salad, 181
Provençal Bean Salad, 189
Radish and Fennel Salad, 190
Salad of Dark Greens, Radicchio,
  and Shrimp, 191
Salami and Cheese Salad, 182
Seafood and Barley Salad, 188
Spinach Salad with Tomato-Shallot
  Dressing, 175
Steamed Breast of Chicken with
  Red-Onion Marmalade, 141
Summer Melon Salad, 184
Tomato and Mozzarella Salad, 183
Warm Finnish Potato Salad, 192

SALMON
Grilled Salmon with Chinese
  Mustard and Leeks, 98
Salmon in Court Bouillon with Herb
  Butter, 99
Sizzled Salmon with Lime Butter,
  101
Sour Cream, Smoked Salmon, and
  Black Caviar Omelet, 23
Vermicelli with Zucchini and
  Smoked Salmon, 59

SALSA
Coriander Salsa, 47

SANDWICHES
Cajun Shrimp Sandwich, 90
Grilled Swordfish Sandwich, 109
Midwest Pork Tenderloin
  Sandwich, 125
Watercress Cucumber Sandwich,
  20

SAUCES and SEASONINGS
Beurre blanc, 108
Caper mayonnaise, 110
Champagne sauce, 86
Cilantro-lime butter, 137
Cinnamon wine sauce, 229
Coriander salsa, 47
Croutons, 36
Cucumber raita, 122
Dill butter, 102
Green-pea and mint sauce, 122
Herb butter, 99
Hollandaise sauce, 149
Mint sauce, 122
Mustard-thyme vinaigrette, 61
Orange syrup, 26
Oriental sauce, 74
Pepper and garlic butter, 116
Red-onion marmalade, 141
Red pepper and garlic sauce, 41
Seafood marinade, 94
Tomato and Pernod butter, 88

SAUSAGE
Sausage and Succotash Soup, 49
Sausages and Oysters, 85
Sweet Sausage with Grapes, 126

SCALLIONS
Sugar-Snap Peas with Scallions,
  152

SCALLOP(S)
Scallop and Bacon Jambalaya, 71
Scallops in White Wine, Shallots,
  and Herbs, 89
Seafood and Barley Salad, 188

SEAFOOD, *see* **FISH** *and also specific
types*

SHELLFISH, *see specific types*

SHORTBREAD
Classic Shortbread, 197
Ginger Shortbread, 198

SHRIMP
Cajun Shrimp Sandwich, 90
Grilled Shrimp with Cilantro, 93
Quick Paella, 67
Salad of Dark Greens, Radicchio,
  and Shrimp, 191
Seafood and Barley Salad, 188
Shrimp Rockefeller, 92
Shrimp with Tuna Fish Sauce, 91
Skewered Shrimp and Scallions, 94

SOUFFLE
Marbleized Pan Soufflé, 232

SOUPS and STOCKS
Brussels Sprouts and Beer-Cheese
  Soup, 35
Chicken Soup with Almonds, 48
Chilled Avocado Soup with
  Coriander Salsa, 47
Chilled Sugar-Snap Pea Soup with
  Mint, 42
Cold Nectarine Soup, 34
Corned Beef and Cabbage Soup, 46
Country Corn Chowder, 43
Court Bouillon, 100
Fennel Soup with Cheese, 44
Orange and Carrot Soup, 61
Peppery Lentil Soup, 46
Sausage and Succotash Soup, 49
Smoky Sweet Potato Soup with
  Sour Cream and Jalapeños, 52

Spring Vegetable Soup, 36
Summer Garden Minestrone, 60
Tomato and Garlic Soup, 40
The Trellis Cheese Soup, 39
Red Snapper Soup, 37
Red Snapper Stew, 38

SPINACH
Spinach Salad with Tomato-Shallot
   Dressing, 175

SQUASH
Chicken Breasts with Summer
   Squash and Yellow Pepper, 140
Vegetable Medley with Green-Pea
   and Mint Sauce, 169

STRAWBERRIES
Minted Strawberries and Sour
   Cream, 237
Riesling-Marinated Strawberries,
   224
White Sangria with Strawberries,
   237

STIR-FRY(IED)
Spicy Stir-Fried Eggplant, 165
Stir-Fried Pork with Broccoli, 124

SWEET POTATOES
Smoky Sweet-Potato Soup with
   Sour Cream and Jalapeños, 52

SWISS CHARD
Savory Swiss Chard Frittata, 28

SWORDFISH
Fish Steaks with Thyme, 105
Grilled Swordfish Sandwich, 109
Grilled Swordfish with Beurre
   Blanc, 107
Swordfish with Tomatoes and
   Basil, 106

TARRAGON
Sautéed Chicken with Tarragon and
   Mushrooms, 139

TOMATO(ES)
Bacon and Tomato Pita Pizzas, 16
Cherry Tomatoes Filled with Goat
   Cheese, 119
Pork Cutlets with Tomato and
   Citrus Sauce, 123
Ravioli with Fresh Tomato and
   Garlic Sauce, 56
Rigatoni with Bacon, Tomato, and
   Ricotta, 62
Saffron Rice with Sun-Dried
   Tomatoes, 70
Sauté of Tomatoes, 158
Summer Garden Minestrone, 60
Swordfish with Tomatoes and
   Basil, 106
Tomato and Garlic Soup, 40
Tomato and Mozzarella Salad, 183
Tomato and Parmesan Cheese
   Topping, 11
Tomato and Pernod Butter, 88

TUNA
Grilled Tuna with Basil and Red
   Peppers, 111
Shrimp with Tuna Fish Sauce, 91
Tuna Steaks Stuffed with Sage and
   Smoked Gouda, 95
Tuna Steaks with Caper
   Mayonnaise, 110

TURKEY
Linguine with Turkey and
   Mushrooms, 60

TURNIP(S)
Vegetable Medley with Green-Pea
   and Mint Sauce, 16

VEAL
Fusilli with Veal and Artichokes, 64
Veal Chops Sauté, 118
Veal Scallops in Lime-Cream
   Sauce, 120

VINAIGRETTE(S), see DRESSING(S)

WAFFLES
Orange and Yogurt Waffles, 26

WALNUTS
Chicken Stuffed with Blue Cheese
   and Walnuts, 142
Maple-Walnut Zabaglione, 233
Sautéed Zucchini with Walnuts, 168
Waldorf Salad, 177
Walnut Fudge Pudding Cake, 205
Walnut Gougere, 17

WATERCRESS
Broiled Lamb Chops on a Bed of
   Sautéed Watercress, 121
Watercress Cucumber
   Sandwiches, 20

WHITE WINE
Broiled Oysters with Shallot Wine
   Sauce, 84
Court Bouillon, 100
Sautéed Chicken with Tarragon and
   Mushrooms, 139
Scallops in White Wine, Shallots,
   and Herbs, 89
White-Wine Ice and Peaches, 208

YOGURT
Orange and Yogurt Waffles, 26
Zabaglione, Maple-Walnut, 233

ZUCCHINI
Bulgur Garden Salad, 187
Eggplant, Zucchini, and Bell-
   Pepper Sauté, 151
Sautéed Zucchini with Walnuts, 168
Skewered Shrimp and Scallions, 94
Summer Garden Minestrone, 60
Vermicelli with Zucchini and
   Smoked Salmon, 59

NOTES

NOTES

NOTES

NOTES

NOTES

NOTES

NOTES